BREACHED!

A Cautionary Tale of Cybersecurity and Intrigue

DAVE MILLIER

Breached!

A Cautionary Tale of
Cybersecurity and Intrigue

ISBN 978-1-61961-378-2

LIONCREST
PUBLISHING

This book is dedicated to my parents, Jim and Jerry Millier, who instilled in me a life-long love of books and reading, and an insatiable thirst for knowledge. Without their love and support over the years, this book would not exist, and I wouldn't be the person I am today. And thanks to my wife, Maria, who puts up with all my crazy ideas, and lets me be me.

CONTENTS

FOREWORD

By Claudiu Popa

In the golden age of radio dramas and electrical transcription discs, some 82 percent of the population would gather around a gloriously massive radio to enjoy weekly entertainment transmitted wirelessly but appearing no less vibrant and exciting than today's high definition television programs. This old-time era of science fiction and mystery storytelling produced such masterpieces and adaptations as Orson Welles' War of the Worlds and more recently Douglas Adams' Hitchhiker's Guide to the Galaxy.

Outstandingly realistic presentations often kept families on the edge of their seats and starred big-name actors whose voices were transmitted and reproduced with relatively high fidelity by the medium of the roaring twenties and the progress made well into the seventies.

In 1978, CBC Radio was the first to broadcast a comedy

programme in stereo with the highly acclaimed Hitchhiker's Guide show that followed the adventures of an Englishman and an alien after an early catastrophe that forced them to adjust to their new reality and frequently learn from galactically authoritative sources of wisdom. The story became a staple of nerd culture for the ensuing decades and continues to be a preferred form of currency for securing *street cred* in IT circles.

While Douglas Adams allegedly stumbled upon the idea for the eminently quotable story while lying drunk in a field in Innsbruck, Dave Millier ostensibly came upon his inspiration by sheer power of observation and a keen desire to educate us, while elucidating the arcane mysteries of all manner of things intangible.

Millier borrows nothing, consciously nor otherwise, from Adams, but their early catastrophes and characters' misadventures captivate the mind and read like most of us imagine the fast paced radio dramas of yesteryear came across.

In Adams' satirical development, Arthur Dent wakes up to discover that his house is about to be demolished and he has only minimal opportunity to delay the inevitable. Moreover, the entire planet is inexorably headed for destruction, illustrating the futility of his earlier effort, but placing him on the path for invaluable experiences and opportunities for galactic adventure with his alien friend, Ford Prefect.

Millier's own doomsday scenario awakens his hapless protagonist with an early morning call that is one of the biggest fears of today's corporate leaders: a disastrous data breach that impacts their organization on every level. In reading Millier's novella, *hitchhikers* are reminded of the powerlessness Arthur Dent would have endured in the early hours of his ordeal, while new audiences will experience the full scale of a modern corporate disaster with fresh eyes.

No reader will be unfamiliar with the security and privacy challenges that populate the front pages of dailies worldwide but most of us are disconnected enough from the urgency of the situations and the proximity of the danger to not internalize everyday events.

Millier's fast-paced, round-by-round account makes tangible the thrill of the discovery and palpable the scale of the challenge facing Tim Smith and Jonathan Williams. What's more, it humanizes the dry accounts of cybersecurity breaches and gives us a taste of the emotions that today pervade boardrooms when businesses face the existential, reputational and financial threats of our tech-dependent society. Breached! succeeds in painting an accurate picture of what goes on behind closed doors when things go off the rails but it can also be enjoyed on a different level that offers a flashback at the intensity that so vividly coloured the imagination of listeners almost a century ago, when radio was the cutting edge technology of the moment.

THE PLAYERS

Orion Corp.: Management Team

Jeff Roberts, Chief Executive Officer/
Chairman of Board of Directors

Doug Thompson, Chief Operating Officer

Alex Martin, Chief Marketing Officer

Tim Smith, Chief Information Officer

Tina Fernandez, Vice President for Communications

Orion Information Technology Department

Tim Smith, Chief Information Officer

Ewan Grant, Operations Manager

Glenn Riles, Network Manager

Jake Peters, Director of Information Security

Scott Stone, Director of Development

Orion Corp.: Outside Consultants

Terry Phillips, Crisis Communications Advisor

Jonathan Williams, DevOps Advisor

Daniel Owens, Managed Service Security Provider Contact

FRIDAY, 5:07 A.M.

Tim Smith looked over at the clock before picking up the phone. His wife Gina was still asleep next to him as it rang. "What the hell is this?" he wondered. He picked up the cordless handset.

"Is this Timothy R. Smith, the CIO at Orion?" a woman asked.

"Ah, yeah," he replied. "Who's this?" The fact that she used his formal first name and middle initial made it ominous.

"This is special agent Janice Parker from the FBI Cybercrimes Unit."

Tim looked over at his still-sleeping wife, and keeping the phone to his ear crept out of the bedroom into the hallway. "Okay. What can I do for you?" he responded, trying not to seem nervous or even bothered.

"I'm the head of our cyber-crime task force. Overnight we've received evidence of a systematic use of stolen credit card information. It's early but the signs are pointing back to a leak from within your company. We feel it's likely your client's information has been breached."

"Oh my goodness," Tim replied. "How many customers appear to be affected?"

"At least thirty thousand from the data dump we found on the Darknet and the initial fraudulent transactions we're seeing," the agent responded. "Do you have any idea where the source could be inside your company for this kind of information leak?"

"Yes...I think I do..."

Two weeks earlier

Tim Smith had never been employed as a Chief Information Officer before, but Orion presented a unique opportunity and was unlike any other place he had worked. In his nearly 15-year career in information technology, he had worked at various business-to-business firms that delivered software-as-a-service offerings and complex consulting solutions. Now he was working for a company that sold burgers. More than that, to be fair: it was a quick service "gastro pub" with items like sweet potato fries and lamb sliders on the menu, and of course lots of craft beer. With nearly 100 locations and $250 million in annual sales, it was a chain on a rapid expansion. The chatter in the financial press indicated that Orion was on track to have an initial public offering of its stock next year.

Tim was poached away while vice president for IT operations at his last firm, which sold software to contractors looking to bid on government procurement projects. He was hesitant about leaving a relatively small pond of an industry he had come to know well for a consumer-facing restaurant chain in another region where his IT skills didn't seem to be a congruent fit. After some convincing from his wife—who swayed him on the opportunity to upgrade their standard of living thanks to the salary increase and stock options he would receive—and some rumination about the chance to manage an IT department from end to end, he called the headhunter back and told him he'd take the interview. A short month later he was installed as Orion's CIO, the first person ever to hold that position in the company's history.

Unlike the world he came from, most of the corporate employees at Tim's new company worked from home, using remote access and cloud services to get their work done. The staff in the office was primarily filled with accountants, marketing, and human resource people. You could still call and ask for any of the executives by their first names and more than likely get their direct connection. Almost all of the company's 2,400 headcount worked in the restaurants and made hourly wages. They were typically part-time and were in school or worked other jobs to make ends meet. This world was new to Tim, including the context in which it placed IT. His last employer was essentially a sales and marketing company, but because it sold software products it placed a significant priority on integrating and relying heavily on IT. After his first week at Orion, Tim quickly realized how naive he had been to assume all large companies valued IT the same way. The other C-level executives seemed to be obsessed with the daily restaurant operations. They were consumed with dissecting the overnight sales numbers that came in from each location. The COO and CFO were always on the road, doing things like negotiating leases for new units or sales contracts for new beers. Even the head of human resources never seemed to be there; she was always out with the regional managers organizing the next round of new hire training.

It wasn't that Orion didn't have any IT systems or products to manage. Tim took the job because he was pleased with how much they had invested in IT to date, and the company's roadmap indicated they planned to do a lot more. All of the restaurants had point of sale terminals for ordering and sales that were considered the best in the industry. Learning the machines was a major part of training for front-of-the-house employees. Furthermore, Orion was in the process of building a mobile application that would allow it to interact directly with patrons. Its functional specifications for customers included paying for their order with the app like you could at Starbucks, loyalty points that would accrue with each order earning them points to redeem towards Orion swag, and the ability to submit comments and pictures of their dining experience for feedback. Tim was confident that with so much of its customer base in the 21-44 year age range with high disposable income, this mobile app would separate Orion from its rivals in the increasingly crowded burger and craft beer market.

But right away Tim could tell that the mobile app project—codenamed Millennial—was in trouble. Orion had made the decision to toggle development between a handful of developers in-house and an outside vendor. There seemed to be no collaboration with anyone else on the IT team, and no thoughts around security or operations. With the public launch date for the app two weeks away from when he arrived, Tim sensed that if something major were going to go wrong it was going to be with Millennial.

He was right.

The warning signs started with the development team, led by an irreverent programmer named Scott Stone. Scott had developed a number of consumer-facing applications before for well-known brands. He came to Orion from a development shop, where Orion's Chief Marketing Officer had employed him as a vendor when he was with his previous company. Scott still had an outsider's approach to the job. He viewed the Millennial project and his development team of six programmers as his own little silo, not to be messed with by others inside the company. Tim was embarrassed when he scheduled an all hands IT meeting his first week at the office and no one from development showed up. As the rest of them talked in broad strokes about information security and system administration, Millennial was like a foreboding storm cloud that didn't get mentioned. The security guy hadn't tested any of it or even supplied input on basic functions, and seemed to have no plan for doing so.

As he drove home Friday night at the end of his first week to the rental apartment he put his family in while they house-hunted in their new city, Tim kept turning over in his mind the dysfunction of the IT department he had been brought in to lead. "No wonder they picked me to be CIO," he thought, almost feeling sorry for himself.

By chance, Tim had a conversation that weekend with an old college classmate who worked in the IT consulting world. Tim meticulously walked Jonathan Williams, who wore the élan of a jet-setting corporate consultant, through the organization structure and IT workflow at Orion after they bumped into each other at a local coffee shop. Jonathan repeatedly nodded as Tim explained how a company as large as Orion had so little engagement with IT. "I know we're about selling burgers and beers," he lamented, "but to treat IT as some irrelevant sideshow? I've never seen that before. We're talking about a company that is getting ready to go public in the next 12 months."

"I have," replied Jonathan. "For most firms whose brands are not related to IT, that's the rule rather than the exception. Every new CIO like you has trouble dealing with this."

This actually made Tim feel a little better. At least he shouldn't take his C-level colleagues' attitude personally. Then his thoughts returned to Millennial.

"What really worries me is a point of sale mobile app we're supposed to take live at the end of next week. We have a one-hundred-thousand-plus email list and even more on social media that we'll be marketing it to so the usage will be heavy. So far its development has been done practically behind closed doors. No one really knows what to expect from it."

“You didn’t tell me about the app!” Jonathan exclaimed. “You’ve never managed development in your past jobs; I have. Managing developers is like herding cats. You don’t understand how difficult these projects are to deliver, especially at the very end. The way you’re going, even if you do any security testing now, you’ll be lucky to bolt on any fixes right before you launch. Anything that affects functionality will be scrapped. It’s a recipe for total disaster.”

Tim had thought he was sufficiently concerned about Millennial until now. He felt embarrassed. It was true he had never worked in development. As a network and then an operations guy, he had been at the center of day-to-day corporate IT activity rather than the building of applications. For the first time in his new CIO role, he felt inadequate skills-wise.

“Look Jonathan,” he responded summoning up humility, “I may need to talk to you again about this. Can we stay in touch?”

“Yes, and call me sooner rather than later. It will make anything I can do more effective. Trust me.”

Tim tried to get on with the rest of the weekend as his family got settled into their new home, but he couldn’t shake the problems on his plate out of his mind.

FRIDAY, 5:35 A.M.

After hanging up with the FBI agent, Tim jumped in the shower instead of calling his boss. He needed to get dressed to go into work anyway, but he also needed a few minutes to think about the crisis that was just dumped on his lap. Orion's most loyal customers' credit card information was being sucked out of their databases into the hands of criminals. Who knew what they were being used for now. Or how this could be stopped. Tim thought of his first tour through the company's restaurants, just a week earlier, to check in on how the mobile apps would interface with the point of sale system at the cash registers. The people coming through the doors to eat lunch or dinner were upper middle class, but they were far from rich. Some of them had young kids. They came in for a good meal at Orion partly because it was less expensive than a full-service restaurant would charge. They thought they were getting good value for a good product. Now their credit cards were stolen, and it was Orion's fault. *How did we get here?* Tim thought to himself.

Tim paused before dialing his CEO Jeff Roberts, and thought over who else needed to be alerted right away. There was the Chief Operations Officer, the head of marketing, definitely the communications lead. Tim dreaded the thought of a conference call with all these personalities. He realized he'd have to project some authority over handling the breach or let these executives, who already had disdain for IT, take charge and make it worse. Tim dialed Jeff Roberts first.

"Jeff, it's Tim. I just got a call from the FBI and they're telling us we've been breached."

Before his boss could even respond with exclamations and expletives, Tim looked down at his iPhone screen and called the COO, Doug Thompson, to add him to the call. After that he meticulously added the other three executives who needed to be involved. All of them picked up, to Tim's surprise.

Tina Fernandez, the VP for communications, was the most difficult to deal with. She strained to downplay the effect of the crisis on Orion as a strategy for deflecting blame. "Tim, what you're saying is that the FBI really isn't sure where the breach entry point is. So it could be with us or it could be with another large company. I don't think we want to accept the blame before we know for sure."

This spin frustrated Tim. He wanted to get off the phone and call Orion's information security provider to figure out what the hell was going on. Helping Tina craft a press release was the least of his concerns. Fortunately, Jeff stepped in. "From what Tim is relating from the FBI, it sounds like they believe the source is us. I don't think we can wait for official confirmation to acknowledge that we believe we have a big problem. Tim, you need to focus on shutting this down now." That was a relief.

Before Tim could even acknowledge Jeff comment, the Chief Marketing Officer Alex Martin interjected. "I just want to make it clear to everyone that we don't know for sure where this could be coming from. It could be from our credit card processor. It could be from our bank. Let's not rush to judgment about the source."

"BS," Tim thought. The odds that it stemmed from their credit card or banking partner was close to nil. Those were institutions that specialized in securing credit card and personal information for a living. They also had much tighter regulatory requirements like PCI-DSS, imposed by the credit card issuers. Alex was trying to preemptively deflect criticism of Millennial, the branded mobile app that he had successfully pushed to go to market over Tim's objections last week.

"Look, everybody get into the office and let's get to work," Jeff announced. "I want to reconvene as a group in two hours to see where we are as a whole. In the meantime every major decision has got to come through me. No outside communications or talking with law enforcement further without me plugged in."

Tim was relieved to get off the call and actually try to start solving the problem. Already dressed, he grabbed his briefcase and headed for the car. He would text his still-sleeping wife later to tell her where he went and why. As he started up the car, that conversation with Jonathan at the coffee shop came back to him. *You're going to bolt on security at the end, if at all*, Jonathan predicted. And of course that's exactly what happened. When Tim tried the mobile application, he quickly realized they had no strong password support at all. The development team downloaded a plug-in off the internet called StrengthenPass, stuck it in place, and over Tim's objections they went live without any testing whatsoever. Tim felt embarrassed that he hadn't heeded Jonathan's next warning to call him sooner rather than later. Maybe that could have headed off the breach. But there was no use playing it backward or feeling sheepish. Tim looked at the clock and wondered if it was okay to call Jonathan yet. He seemed like a guy who got up early—what the hell.

FRIDAY, 7:25 A.M.

There was no answer from Jonathan, or from Daniel Owens, Tim's contact at SecureSOC, the managed service information security provider Orion contracted with. Same with Jake Peters, the information security director at Orion who Tim had barely spoken with the past two weeks.

It was almost time for the meeting with Jeff and the rest of the C-suite, and Tim didn't want to walk in empty-handed. He sent Jonathan a text message: "We've been hacked. It's bad... at least 30 thousand credit cards and customer records out in wild. Can we talk asap?"

Tim slumped back in his desk chair and cycled through all the things that had already gone wrong with his response to the news from the FBI hours earlier. He should never have gotten the other executives on the phone with Jeff; they only made it worse. Each one was probably off formulating their own response plan that could undercut fixing the actual breach, which was all that Tim cared about at the moment. He should have just spoken with Jeff directly—that would have enabled him to take charge and not have to compete for airtime with his CEO. Instead he let himself fall into the role Orion carved out for its CIO as an ancillary figure.

About to doze off after closing his eyes, Tim was startled back to attention by his phone: a call back from Jonathan.

"Got your text. Sounds like you have a big problem on your hands buddy!"

"No kidding," Tim replied. "The FBI's involved, it's crazy. I don't know what we're going to do. I just want to find and plug this breach and make sure our customers are okay, but we don't even have a plan. Honestly, I'm not sure it's safe for our restaurants to open at 11 a.m. today."

"This has got to be that mobile app you told me about," Jonathan said. "I remember you were planning on collecting a ton of credit card info and PII and had a big list to market it to. Also that security wasn't even introduced a few weeks out. That's a deadly combination."

"Exactly," said Tim. "We just went through our managed service provider per company protocol. They barely talked with the development team, or even with me. Of course, I tried to delay the app launch and no one here would let me. The product they bolted on deals with weak passwords—StrengthenPass, looks like a terrible choice. From what I could find on the internet it's typically used for internal software projects, it has no place inside an enterprise mobile application.

"StrengthenPass is the worst!" Jonathan exclaimed. "I've run across so many companies—usually the ones farthest away from anything to do with software—that decide to make whatever software they need in house and then slap that product on to call it secure because they got it in the bargain bin of what they went looking for."

"Look, Jonathan. I really need your help. I don't know what we're going to do. It's beyond just the hacking itself. I don't have the authority here to take on the people who put us in this situation. If I don't get another voice in here with me it's going to be over, I might as well just resign on the spot."

"Whoa, calm down, buddy," Jonathan answered. "Don't do anything rash. I might be able to help you with this problem. But I'd have to clear out projects I'm working on with clients, plus you know I don't come cheaply. Make sure you guys can afford me first."

"Jonathan, I'm not going to negotiate with you. We'll pay your asking price. I'm about to head into an executive committee meeting and I'm going to tell them we're hiring you. If they say no, I'm out. I don't want to fight this fire without someone by my side that knows what they're doing."

"Tim, I appreciate the trust you have in me. And I want to help you. I was about to board a flight home from a client visit, but I can rebook to get to where you are. Best I can probably do is be at your office mid-afternoon today. We can go from there.

Until then, I'll be out of contact because this crappy regional airline I'm boarding has no Wi-Fi."

"Thank you, Jonathan. You have no idea how much this means to me. Talk to you soon."

Another call—the first incoming one to his cell phone that morning since Tim's pleasant chat with the Mountie computer crimes agent. It was Daniel, his contact at Securesoc, finally returning his voicemail.

"Sorry for the late response," Daniel said. "I've already been in touch with Ewan and we took the Millennial app offline. Apparently Scott did some research online and found out that the *StrengthenPass* product has a bunch of security holes in the version you implemented, we figure that's how the bad guys got in and the information got stolen. The agent who you talked to called me too. This is bad—we're going to have to keep records of everything we do with you guys from here on out for any potential criminal investigation or civil action, including all correspondence. I've never been involved in anything like this before, it's unsettling."

Tim was stunned that his managed security guy seemed more concerned about himself than his client at a time like this, but he knew that in stressful times everyone was out to cover their own ass. Both Orion and Securesoc would surely have to talk more with the authorities in the days ahead, and give them a step-by-step walkthrough what they'd done to shut down the application and limit any further access to the Millennial application data. But for now Tim had to do his own version of forensics work.

“Daniel, can you just level with me—how exactly do you think the hackers got in and how did the application become that porous in the first place?”

“I don’t really want to speculate on something that important, Tim. But if I had to guess, with the limited information I have so far I’d have to say Ewan may be right and there’s a security hole that was introduced when they installed that StrengthenPass plugin to try to improve security right before they went live. “

Daniel was hesitant to offer too much speculation, which Tim figured made sense, he didn’t want to get himself or Securesoc into any trouble, and Tim couldn’t fault him for that, it looked like Orion had plenty of that itself to deal with at the moment.

With that, Tim got off the phone and headed for Jeff Roberts’ corner office, ready to tell them about their newest consultant.

For the first time since that wakeup call in the darkness of early morning, Tim felt a little bit better. The bleeding looked like it could be contained with the app offline. They had bought themselves some breathing room, time to do a thorough analysis of what went wrong, hopefully implement some changes and then things could get back under control. The company would own up to the problem publicly as soon as it faced inquiries from the media and show it was committed to putting its customers first. He took a deep breath and bounded into Jeff’s office prepared to debrief the executive committee on his agreement with Jonathan.

As Tim stepped in to the spacious suite, he was surprised to see a stranger standing where Jeff would stand in front of his mahogany desk, addressing the group around the conference table in the front of the room. "...the most important thing is to not deflect attention from the pain point itself," the man was saying.

"Tim, welcome" Jeff said from his seat at the table. "Come take a chair. This is Terry Phillips, our crisis consultant. Terry's worked in two government administrations doing press relations and has advised automotive companies when things go wrong. Maybe you know him from MSNBC. Terry's setting the course for us on how to steer out of this Millennial app meltdown."

Tim took another deep breath and looked at the consultant. He was about 50, and like a lot of "authorities" seemed to be trying to look younger, with an open collar shirt under his blazer and thick-framed eye-glasses. Tim had seen him on cable news before, giving talking points on the President's speeches. Now he was at Orion's headquarters, seemingly in charge of the place, dictating the strategy they were all supposed to be collaborating on.

"The thing is," Terry continued, "the public is so unfamiliar with cyber-attacks—just because there haven't been that many of them—that it doesn't really know who to blame when one of them happens. Is it law enforcement for not doing its job? Is it the tech companies that this stuff all gets processed through? Or is it the communist government or military in China? In the polling we've done in the past we tend to find that blame gets spread around evenly at the beginning and then gets reallocated once the media has had a chance to report on it. So that really means these next couple days are going to be crucial in telling our narrative. We've got to decide who we want to point the finger at for the media, who's the bad guy here?"

Tim couldn't believe that what was happening to Orion was now being distilled into a political "narrative" for packaging to the press. The bad guys were whoever hacked into Orion's customers' information. Maybe they were in China, but it didn't matter right now. It wasn't as important as *stopping* the attack and making sure the rest of their clients' confidential information was protected.

Terry had drawn up overlapping circles with each potential "bad guy" on a white board. Tina, the communications director, was making lists of staff assignments to dig into each one and make the case that the Millennial meltdown could be pointed at them. While everyone else stayed engrossed in Terry's performance, Tim quietly tapped Jeff on the shoulder and asked to pull him out of the meeting.

"What's up," Jeff asked?

"Look, Jeff, I have to level with you," Tim responded. "This meeting is so far removed from what matters in shutting down the breach that I can't partake in it. We haven't even plugged the hole. For all we know, what was happening as we slept last night is still happening to our customers. We can't have a PR response as a substitute for stopping the breach!

"Tim, we pay this guy ten grand a month to swoop in whenever something bad happens. For the first time, he's got a project to take on. He's had experience before putting out fires at public brands like ours. Unlike the rest of us, he's been through this type of thing before."

"Jeff, my point is we're on separate tracks. Terry wants to win the PR battle. I want to identify and solve this problem. You hired me as the head of IT not only to make sure everything works, but also to make it secure. I need to have the latitude to do that at a time like this when the company's survival is at stake."

"You think it's that bad, huh?"

"The FBI woke us up this morning. We've got tens of thousands of people enrolled through that app, and all that data is out in the wild. You want to take this company public. I don't see how we could do that if we don't make things right with our customers."

"Well, what do you want to do separate from this?"

"Two things: first, I want to bring in a consultant I trust. He does crisis response like Terry but instead of spinning he actually fixes the underlying problem. Second, I want your support to go through and find out where the bodies are buried in IT. Before this happened, I could sense things were screwed up, now we have proof. When my consultant gets here I want to take him through a tour of everything that's messed up so something like this doesn't happen again. People are going to bitch and moan about it when I start questioning them, and I need you to back me up on this."

"I'll back up your authority to improve things clearly dysfunctional," Jeff responded, "but I'm not keen on bringing in some expert consultant to do a major revamp. What can someone really do in the middle of an emergency to fix something at a growing company like ours? This isn't the time to do that kind of stuff—I'd rather we stay in firefighting mode and take care of this emergency. Maybe down the road in the next fiscal year you bring in this guy when we have a budget for it."

Tim's slumped his shoulders. He was expecting Jeff to object to his push for authority rather than the idea of bringing Jonathan in. With this quack down the hall on retainer for ten grand a month it didn't seem like a big deal to bring in one more body, and now Jeff was invoking concerns about expertise and budgets. Plus, he was pessimistic of actually addressing the IT status quo that led to this mess, which was totally out of sync with Jeff's usual optimistic-style-CEO nature. He decided to challenge this head on.

"Jeff, I get the sense that you don't feel great about fixing IT here. That you just want to fix this mess and get on with life. That's an understandable sentiment with all you've got on your plate, especially with an IPO in the works. But let me tell you, it's going to happen again if we don't look under the hood of all aspects of IT and see what's really happening here—security, development, operations, we need to look at everything. It may be the mobile app today but it will be something else in the future, whether it's the next generation of that app or some other location we store customer or employee data. We're loaded with sensitive inadequately protected information and it's sitting there vulnerable to the outside world. I've only been here two weeks but that's long enough to see there's a real problem and know it's a series of ticking time bombs. The first one just went off."

Jeff paused in reflection, seemingly stunned by Tim's impassioned warning. Until now he had seen Tim as a smart, capable executive but not someone who he thought about in any terms of political heft. Now that was changing. Tim had a point of view of the company that was foreign to Jeff and the rest of the C-suite. It was an alarming point of view to hear spoken out loud. Tim seemed to be staking his reputation on it, too.

"Okay, okay. I get your point, Tim. Go ahead and formulate a plan to restructure IT so we're safe and functional. I can't deal with a repeat of this morning. Hell, I don't even know when the bleeding is going to stop from today. You take on whatever it is that caused it to happen in the first place. But do you really need to bring in that consultant? Can't you lead this yourself?"

Tim had to admire Jeff's last-ditch zeal for cost saving, but that was made easier by the confidence he had in selling Jonathan.

"Jeff, this is going to *save* us money because in the end we'll make our IT systems work better and won't need to hire more people to fix the mess they've created. This guy, Jonathan Williams, he specializes in this stuff—fixing dysfunctional IT programs at companies. He's written books about it, things like making development and operations work in tandem with each other. Besides his intellect, it's going to be more effective to have an outside voice like his working with me to diagnose everything that's wrong and providing guidance on how to address it permanently. If it's just me making demands it might come off as a power trip. I want complete buy-in from our staff."

"I get that. Okay, you can have your guy. But don't broadcast it to anyone back there"—pointing to his office—"otherwise every other department leader is going to want their specialty consultant. This is a deal between you and me; let's keep it need-to-know."

"You bet, Jeff. I promise you won't be disappointed by this."

"Okay, let's get back to work."

FRIDAY, 3:35 P.M.

The hours of waiting for Jonathan to arrive felt to Tim like days, not because of any boredom but because of the chaotic and unilateral reactions by his subordinates. They were all in various states of shock when he gathered them in his office. Glenn Riles the network/systems manager, fanatically wanted to roll out a new server because that's what he thought every company was supposed to do at a time like this. A new server was deemed the best way to break apart from the old infected program and prevent any further intrusion. He also wanted to tinker with the network architecture to finish a performance upgrade he had started last week, which to Tim at this point seemed like rearranging the deck chairs on the Titanic.

Ewan Grant, the operations manager, was perplexed that he had no visibility into the system and couldn't tell if anyone was on the network at the moment or whether or not they needed to be locked out. He also had store managers calling him non-stop, worried that their point of sale machines' would be impacted with Millennial taken off line in the aftermath of the breach. Without those registers they wouldn't be able to do any business. Ewan couldn't see what was going on in all these systems and could only look at each one individually, making his check-up fruitless. "I can't just shut down all the systems because one has gone fatally wrong," he told Tim. "Our business model depends on most of them working. I have to turn the POS application back on so the restaurants can open, we just won't turn Millennial back on until we sort this out."

Tim was somewhat surprised initially that Ewan had so little visibility into his network and systems, but then after a moment of reflection decided that no, he really wasn't that surprised after all. Based on everything he'd seen so far in his first two weeks on the job, this just seemed par for the course.

Scott, Orion's lead in development who had seemingly staged a group boycott of Tim's first all-hands IT meeting, was showing no better of an attitude. He dismissed out of hand the possibility that the vulnerability point was in the code he and his team had built, pointing to his research on StrengthenPass as being the likely culprit. At the same time though he complained that they were working under a ridiculous time constraint to ship the program. He told Tim—in front of Ewan—that he wanted authority to go into the operations deployment logs and try to pinpoint where the intrusion happened. "That's ridiculous," Ewan snapped back. "You have no understanding of rollout or logging!"

"Yes I do," said Scott. "And since you have no clue how an

application interacts with the real world it's going to be up to me to solve this."

"Don't be absurd," Ewan followed. "All you do over there is sit behind your lines of code and tinker around with bells and whistles on products that will impress the people upstairs. You have no clue how to fix this."

"Guys, enough!" Tim shouted. His day was barely started and already he was too tired to referee this fight, and it was pointless to have since no one in front of him had any idea of how to fix the breach and anything they did could make it worse. An additional alarming detail was that Jake, the security guy, was present but totally sidelined from this conversation, as if the other three considered him a nonfactor and were going to do whatever they wanted to do without his agreement or input.

Tim finally excused himself to head over to the airport and pick up Jonathan. It brought a sigh of relief, not just to be out of the hothouse of the office, but also knowing that the 30-minute return ride would give the two of them a chance to talk privately before he reentered the fray. Tim was prepared to give him the blow-by-blow of everything that had happened at Orion from early that morning, right through to the melee in his office that afternoon, but Jonathan didn't need to hear it. Instead, his mind was already humming with the litany of things he wanted to tackle. He was simultaneously concerned with plugging the breach and making sure it couldn't happen again.

"One thing I've been thinking about is your SDLC—your

software development lifecycle," Jonathan said. "That's where the vast majority of vulnerabilities get introduced into applications these days, at the software level. The company is focused on delivering cool features to its customers, the developers are focused on the functionality, application performance, and of course time to develop, and no one really considers security until the last minute. And it's because so many more companies like Orion have their own custom software that they end up painting big targets on their backs. These days, custom development is the bane of many companies I work with. A lot of times I'm being brought in to help them deal with security issues, and only after a breach has occurred."

"Tell me about it," Tim replied. "Everyone wants to be in the software business these days, even if they're like us and their core business is burgers and French fries."

"Exactly. The SDLC is supposed to at least streamline the process for companies that choose to build software. The idea is that when you build an application, there are steps that you follow. First you have to plan, and security needs to be sitting at the table from Day One. It's crucial to have information security represented at the inception of the application, throughout development, all the way through to final testing and deployment. Having them involved in the planning step will ensure security isn't skipped or forgotten when starting to plan the application. The software developers typically aren't thinking about authentication, about roles-based access control, about how they're going to write the code securely. There are very, very few companies who actually bring a security person in at the beginning, which is why we're seeing such a significant increase in corporate breaches."

"Jonathan, I know what you mean: even at the companies I worked for in the past whose sole product was software as a service—those firms mostly just focused on shipping new features to clients rather than making sure it was secure. Security was an afterthought in the SDLC, if it existed at all."

"There you go. What normally happens instead is that those developers and their bosses spend all of their time thinking about functionality questions such as, 'What is the application going to do? Who is the intended audience? What does it need to look like? What are the aesthetics? What's the language we're going to use?' And then at the very end of the software development life cycle, once they've built this impressive application, they're getting ready to go to production and say, 'Oh, you know what? We should do some type of security testing just to make sure there are no security issues with our application.'

"Well, guess what: almost invariably there are problems with the application. So what do these developers do now? Do they go back to the beginning and start all over again and design and code it the right way with security contemplated from the start? No. What they do is *bolt on* security. It's a crude addition at the very end intended to augment rather than embed security in the application."

"Consider a house and its foundation. When building a house, if you start with a solid foundation, everything you build on top of it relies on that base to keep it supported. If you ignore the foundation and you just built the house? Not so solid, right? Your house is vulnerable settling, shifting, or some other catastrophe because it doesn't have that solid foundation. Same logic applies to any application. Hackers can get around bolted-on security a lot easier than security that's instituted as part of a well thought-out pre-planned foundation which includes security."

"You're talking about the only world I know," Tim responded. "In my experience, *bolt on* wasn't even a pejorative the way you've used it. It's just the standard move of adding security on at the end of the process."

"Exactly," Jonathan said. "They do it because that's the easy way out. They ignore security for as long as possible then worry about it for a second just before shipping. The right way to do it is having that security guy sitting at the table, not just at the very beginning, but also throughout the entire software development life cycle. So they're not just testing at the very end, they've got security included in the architecture, they're thinking about security when they're writing code, they're doing incremental security testing at every stage in the development process. Once they finish building the application, they can be assured that its far more secure using this method than if they had just done it the same way everyone else does and bolted on security to address any problems they find at the end."

"They've also gained a competitive advantage because most companies are not aware of the risks of bolting on after development is fundamentally complete. Like I said, a significant number of larger companies are now doing their own development. They're not relying on off-the-shelf software because there is a really good pool of developers out there that can build custom solutions that allow the company to get exactly what they need to solve a business problem or problems, without having to change the way they do things because the software they bought doesn't do what they need or only works in a specific way. But most companies are not software development companies—just the way Orion is a gastropub or whatever the hell you guys call it. Therefore they're not software development savvy. So they hire somebody to come in to build a software development team for them or they just outsource the development to another company entirely. And it can be a rather routine and casual connection to the group they are bringing in. 'I worked with these guys before on a joint project and they made a nice piece of software for the client,' a senior manager might say. The hiring decision is made without regard to security, and they don't really teach security to developers in school.'"

"What do you mean they don't teach security to developers in school?" Tim asked.

"Oh yeah, I almost forgot you're an operations guy not a developer," Jonathan grinned. "The schools teach them about the language and structure and reuse of code. But reuse of code is one of the greatest points of security vulnerability because if the code is weak and you reuse it over and over and over, which is what most developers do, then you're re-introducing the same problem into your application a hundred times over rather than just having it in one spot. Reuse itself contributes to weaknesses.

"It is part of the larger disconnect from security that results with so many firms in the software development business even though that's not their core competency. They are prone to taking the shortcuts described above because they lack the experience and expertise to plan software life cycle development. They think that they're squared away by handing that off to the developers—but the developers aren't thinking any more about security than the companies themselves are."

"What is the best way to test for security once the application is done?" Tim inquired. "The testing at least could have aborted the launch of Millennial. I noticed that password problem, they tried to fix it with a crappy plugin piece of code, and now it looks like they did no testing or validation and just went live."

"When a piece of software is finished there are two types of tests that typically take place: static code analysis and dynamic code analysis. In the static world, the tester would get a copy of the source code and then could run a bunch of tools against it and could review the results. If the tester is actually a developer he could look for known weaknesses. If your guys at Orion did anything, I'm guessing at most they did a little bit of static testing, but likely just went through the motions.

"In the dynamic code analysis world, you're actually running the application and trying to get the application to do things that the developer didn't design it do, exposing it to queries and user actions he never thought it could be exposed to. It's a test on the live system itself rather than an offline test. *That* is what might have saved your app.

"There needs to be testing by the developers as they're building the software all along, not necessarily every day, but once a week or once a month goes a long way to finding bugs and security flaws as they get introduced to the code, allowing the developer to quickly address them. Running some type of static code review ensures they're not putting insecure code in their software because if they reuse it, they're just spreading the same problem around. Then they also have that periodic dynamic code review where somebody is actually testing the functionality of the application to make sure that there's not inadvertent insecure code resulting in flaws in the application which can lead to information leakage."

Tim's thoughts crept back to that first week at Orion when people in the IT department just talked in broad, almost nonsensical terms when he queried them about security for the app. Or how none of the developers came to the first meeting he organized. They must have been using endless lines of bad code, and there appeared to be no formalized process for checking it before rolling out Millennial.

"Another element you have to fix is standard imaging," Jonathan continued. "It's another challenge very similar to developing applications that a CIO like you is faced with when trying to simplify his IT infrastructure. Just like with the software development life cycle, most companies are in the habit of letting security threats walk right through their doors because of the way they set up and deploy their computers.

"It used to be that if a firm had 1,000 employees, it would set up that many computers, one at a time, with each computer getting loaded with Microsoft Office and its features like Word and Excel. But today we start with one computer, build it, harden it to make it more secure, and then make a 'copy' of that PC. We call this the "gold image". The same approach should be used when setting up the company's servers. The applications are all set up and tuned properly to fit the company's and the user's needs. That template on the computer is the equivalent of what the music industry uses to press copies of CDs or MP3s once an album is finished. In the IT world, they create a gold image and that's the copy they're going to use when you install any new desktop computer. It's saved on the server, so every time they roll out a new desktop or a new Windows server, it's always going to be that image.

"The problem is that when you install Windows by default, especially on the server side, there can be a bunch of things installed that you're never going to use. And those things may be applications running that are listening for types of connections from the outside world, and because the operators are never going to use them, they're not really thinking about them. They're not necessarily patching them or updating them as the system is being managed over time, so these are ripe for security weakness.

"The right approach with the gold image is not to just set up all the applications required, but to do a security test against the template before it's ever used. You disable or delete any unnecessary services, shut down things that aren't supposed to be running, and test it again. Once you confirm that only the applications and services that you expect are running you would create your gold image. Then ideally when the images are used to stage new PCs and new servers, the only things that are running are the things that you know are supposed to be running. If you build a gold image but don't do any system hardening and then reuse it over and over again you're simply reintroducing the same security vulnerabilities every time.

"The gold image may have been based upon Windows 2012. But it's now Windows 2012 R2. So if the image was made a year or two ago, which is not unusual when a new operating system comes out, a company is using an image that has security weaknesses in it that Microsoft fixed a year or a year-and-a-half ago but hasn't been updated on the gold image to reflect that fix."

"So what would you do differently with the gold image?" Tim interjected.

"The operations team should be taking this operating system, putting the image on it, patching it, updating it, and then making a *brand new* gold image. They should be doing that every time they update their operating system, whether it's once every month, every three months, once every six months, or once a year. But most companies don't do it. They do it when a new operating system comes out. Or they do it when they have a new application that they want to provide to all their users. But otherwise they very rarely go back and update that gold image.

"And the same logic applies in the virtualized world where it's even worse. In the old physical world, you had a CD or a DVD, and that was the source for the installation. You actually saw the physical machine you were setting up—remember those days? But now in the virtual world the gold image is not even a physical thing. It's not on a CD or DVD anymore, it's just a piece of code stored somewhere. It's a piece of software that's sitting there waiting to be taken for a spin. It's an image of a server or a PC, and so every time you turn a new server or PC on in a virtualized environment, you're taking that image that has security weaknesses in it and reintroducing it into the network over and over again. It's reintroducing whatever vulnerabilities were in that image. Just the way a developer reuses insecure code, in the case of the gold image the network and the operating system folks are doing the same thing.

"Tim, think about which employees are working on computers. Isn't it almost everyone in the company? It's the folks working at the registers. It's the manager in the office after the shift. It might even be the cooks behind the line getting the order tickets. Even though you're a burger place, you're like most businesses these days where just about every employee is using a computer. At your corporate headquarters their people who work with Excel or Word or Photoshop or whatever enables them to do their job on a daily basis. Now when there are normal updates for those applications, they know about it because it happens on their screen, usually prompts them to do something, and they usually do it or ignore it, depending on the user. But it's not the same for security updates. Microsoft does its security updating on a monthly basis—usually on the second Tuesday of each month, Patch Tuesday. Logically speaking, when all those new patches come out, the operations and server teams should be firing up the gold images, applying all those new patches, and creating a brand new copy of the gold image.

"Unfortunately that usually doesn't happen. The logic is often, 'Oh well. We'll just use the current one and when we're running it, if it's installing three or four or five or six months' worth of patches, no big deal.' Meanwhile, they put a new system online and it's got all these vulnerabilities that have been there all along. They're assuming it's going to get patched but maybe it's a month away before the company actually runs through the patch cycle. Not every company is going to patch it automatically as soon as they plug it in. Most companies turn off automatic patching for their servers, so they're waiting and expecting somebody to actually log in and patch the system or use some type of patch management tool to push the patches out. This ultimately can lead to making the servers vulnerable to attacks because of standard imaging. It doesn't have to be this way."

"So just like with testing, you're saying the patching has to be done regularly to avoid a meltdown?"

"Exactly. Treat these operating system security updates as serious as creating a new gold image—because that's what you're doing. You're making sure that everyone everywhere is getting the updated security and no computer is left without it. Don't let them become stale and fall behind without updating the gold images."

Tim was so lost in their conversation he had to reorient his eyes to the road above the steering wheel of his Ford Explorer. They were cruising on the highway with no other cars in sight—that midday lull before evening rush hour commences. He thought about how this was a much better place for such an important conversation than the Orion offices.

Jonathan continued, "Even once security is in place, it won't be effective if there are ways for users and systems to work around it. That's a problem when it comes to network architecture. It's very common to see people routing traffic around firewalls or around security tools that are put in place because the thought is, 'It's impacting performance, it's slowing things down' or even 'I just need to get this online and it isn't working, I don't have access to the firewall, and the security guy is gone so let's plug directly into the Internet for now and we'll move it later.' And, of course, later never comes and the unplugging or reintroducing the proper security controls never happens."

"That mentality is especially prevalent in a consumer-facing company like ours," Tim said. "Our employees have thousands of customers a day to serve—waiting to make sure something is secure isn't really a habit, and I'm sure for many of them it would be considered a liability, preventing them from doing their jobs."

"Exactly," Jonathan answered. "It's the same issue with firewall changes. People make changes on the firewall because they're trying to get a new program working. They're trying to get something new up and running. Maybe for you guys it's a new timesheet application.

"Typically in a firewall, information security will try to restrict as much as it can of what the users can actually do. Firewalls are made up of a bunch of rules dictating what we want our users and systems to be able to do and just as importantly to not do. The rule that often gets handed down is an 'any' rule where they'll say, 'We'll allow users to do anything for the moment so we can test this application or ensure this new service is working, and then we'll restrict it later.' But later never comes. Meanwhile, things are far more exposed on that particular system than was intended. It could have been that they were only supposed to be allowed web access to enter their hours and days worked, but with the any rule in place somebody from the outside could connect through to a system that they weren't supposed to connect to. In this case, the firewall is just acting as a glorified router, it's not really protecting anything.

"Security testing *can* find these things, but if a firm is not doing regular assessments or, as is usually the case, is only doing annual testing, that vulnerable open port could sit there for a long time, up to a full year before the audit. They could put the server online the day after they've done their annual testing and it could sit there for an entire year with those ports and services exposed to the outside world. TCP ports are what 'listen' from a system such as a server on the network and allow connections into the device. When unnecessary ports are open and waiting for people to connect to them, they may be exposing information or providing a way of accessing the system that shouldn't be there. They're like doors swung wide open. The same logic applies for services. When an operating system is installed, a bunch of services are turned on by default. If you don't need them running, they should be turned off. Otherwise each one could have security vulnerabilities that are being introduced for no reason.

"Take the example of web applications firewalls, or WAF, and intrusion prevention systems, or IPS. These systems are usually inline, meaning all the traffic flows through them before it actually gets to the application. So each one of those systems that was put in place introduces some type of latency and could introduce some level of performance issues. Often it's the network administrator getting a complaint that the network is slow. Everybody always hears about the network being slow. But the network people respond, 'It's not my problem, it's your application' or 'It's not my problem, it's your server.' There's always a finger pointing exercise trying to identify whose problem it is instead of agreement on what the problem is and then determining out how to resolve it.

"'What could be the bottleneck?' everyone wonders. They look at the network diagram and traffic flow into and through the network to try and identify systems in place between the application and the Internet that could be slowing it down. And then they try to eliminate each of those. Every one of them is a potential bottleneck. 'Let's just eliminate any of the bottlenecks until the application is running at the performance level we want it to', the thinking goes. So they turn off port spanning, or shut off the IPS, or reroute the traffic around it. Now everything is working fine. But they've turned off logging. Visibility is compromised. They can't do any monitoring for intrusion prevention.

"Exactly," responded Tim. "It's all about performance instead of security. People just want to see something working the way they think it's supposed to work. It's against their instinct to follow the rules if they don't conform to their way of thinking."

"If you think about what a firewall does normally, it's like a security guard," Jonathan continued. "Something comes to it and the security guard says, 'Yes, you can come in,' or 'No, you can't.' A security guard isn't looking to see what you're doing once you get in. He's just stopping you at the entrance and saying, 'Are you allowed to come in or are you not?' A web application firewall, on the other hand, or an intrusion prevention system, it's looking to see what you're planning on doing before it lets you on the network, and even once you're allowed in it's watching to see what are you actually doing. It's like a video surveillance camera for your network. It's actually watching to see what activity you're doing.

"Most administrators rely on the firewall at the edge to make the decision whether traffic can or can't come in. But most traffic nowadays is Secure Sockets Layer—web application traffic. The secure connection prevents the firewall from seeing what you're trying to do. All it can do is say, 'Yes, you can come in.' or 'No, you can't.' Once that SSL traffic is inside, if there's not proper monitoring in place, we have no idea what you're actually doing. That's where those other systems come into play to help review and validate what's happening. But they come into play at a cost and that cost typically is performance because they have to stop the traffic and verify that the traffic really is supposed to do what it's trying to do before they allow it past."

"It's like a traffic cop," Tim said.

"Right, just in better disguise," replied Jonathan. "A web application firewall normally looks to the outside world like it's the actual application. When your customer is paying for their lunch with their bank debit card, for instance, it goes through a web application firewall first, and it verifies the types of traffic they're trying to do or that the communication is legitimate, and then it proxies the connection on to the actual application.

"But that can introduce an extra one millisecond or even an extra second depending on how many other customers are also trying to use the application at the same time. So each one of those layers can add a level of latency. That's why security tools are in place but in many cases get turned off, or just taken off the network entirely, because it's deemed unacceptable for performance."

"The company wants that customer's business more than it wants to protect that customer's information," Tim said.

"Exactly," responded Jonathan. "Every time a company adds in a layer of security or an extra type of security, there's always a potential that it's going to slow things down. It's no different than a trip through the airport. We expect better security when we fly, so we're willing to suffer through extra time. It should be the same thing online. The customer will be okay and in almost all cases won't even notice if it takes an extra second to connect to our website. But maybe your network manager thinks the users won't be happy and orders the security layer stripped away. That's the challenge the information security folks are always trying to work around. So believe it or not, Tim, I have a lot of sympathy for the folks at Orion."

Yeah, well wait 'til you see this sorry lot, Tim thought. Jonathan's contrast between performance and sacrifice made sense though, especially in a harried business like quick-service burgers and beer where making money was in many ways dependent upon speed. Tim had to convince everyone with a stake in the customer service process—which was pretty much everyone in leadership at the company and each unit—that it was worth waiting an extra second or two for firewalling that actually did its job, not just some minimal level of security that realistically speaking wasn't helping make anything secure. He needed to show them after this breach that it wasn't just about performance: Orion's customers were handing over their information when they installed and configured the new mobile app, and every time they paid with their credit or debit card. It was the company's responsibility to protect this PII without letting it into the wild. That's where Millennial broke down: it was built around functionality without any appreciation for security.

They were making their way to the off-ramp for Orion's exit. Jonathan continued to his next urgent topic.

"There is traditionally one other way for a CIO like you and his information security charges to learn about major security lapses besides through a breach."

"Oh, do you mean instead of the catastrophe that's happened today? That's a nice example of Monday morning quarterbacking" Tim joked.

"Oh, there's going to be a lot of Monday morning quarterbacking while I'm here working for you," Jonathan volleyed back. "What I'm talking about is regular internal reviews. Typically, an internal security audit is only done once a year. What does that mean? It's essentially a snapshot of the firm's security position. It's a picture of what's happening on the network and with the company's systems at a point in time. What comes back is a lagging indicator because the data has been organized and analyzed over a period of several weeks, but prepared after that snapshot was taken."

"That how it's been done at every place I've been—everyone anticipates what that audit is going to come back with," Tim said.

"Consider the potential changes that can occur during that time period between when the audit is being prepared and the audit report is delivered. Things that may have been found in the audit to be issues may be gone by then. But just as likely, there are new vulnerabilities that have been added to the network that information security is not even aware of. Why not? The auditor ran the scan and the day after the scan the developers rolled out a new version of the software. The vulnerability gets introduced the next day just like that. With annual, snapshot auditing that vulnerability could be there as long as the next 364 days until next year."

"Okay, Tim stepped in. "But like I said everywhere I've worked—and I've never been a CIO before so I wasn't the one who decided this—we did it that way. It was like a ritual in IT. What's the alternative?"

"I'm glad you asked: ongoing or perpetual auditing and reviews is the answer. It's akin to going to the dentist for a teeth cleaning regularly rather than just when the plaque builds up. Instead of once a year the internal audit is done much more often, ideally monthly or worst case quarterly. The methodology of the audit is the same but it's done on a frequent and regular basis. Two things change with this. Obviously, the latency period for vulnerabilities gets cut way down, but this works in the company's favour. Instead of getting a huge list of security problems once a year and then having to tackle 12 months' worth of issues, you get a small manageable list of issues that can be prioritized and tackled right away. You also gain the ability to track your progress and demonstrate that you're actually doing something that is having an impact by reducing the overall risk to Orion. You also get an idea of what's happening over time. You see the changes affecting important things throughout the year, not just from one day if you're doing annual auditing. That offers a chance to identify root causes—something never afforded by the snapshot audit. Ongoing auditing and reviewing provides empirical learning about the big issues and uncovers opportunities to improve, such as the gold image, that demand regular attention.

"Instead of creating more work for information security and the auditors, ongoing auditing actually involves *less* heavy lifting because of its frequency. Because networks and systems are dynamic and therefore in a state of constant change, a company may have hundreds or even thousands of findings; this translates to a whole new set of work that has to be scheduled on top of their normal workload. Maybe the company is rolling out a new product or is moving to a new data center.

When the results from the annual audit are presented, it creates chaos. Is your IT team going to drop everything they're working on to deal with the vulnerabilities from the audit? They'll get to them when they get to them, which is why the average time now for a vulnerability to exist on a network before it's identified and addressed is *over 200 days*! And even after they're aware of it, most companies take at least 45 days to remediate the problem, which is simply unacceptable. We have the knowledge and capabilities to deal with these issues far more effectively, most companies simply don't have the motivation or the inclination, they can't seem to relate it to the devastating impact a breach can have on their organization when they leave these vulnerabilities unresolved."

"Then why do most firms do the snapshot assessment?" Tim asked.

"Because it gives them a checkmark for compliance, just like other auditing requirements, whether it's in finance or consumer data. If the standard requires them to do a financial audit once a year, then they're inclined to do the security audit annually as well. But the hazards of this approach stem from the principle described earlier: compliance follows security, not the other way around. Getting the compliance checkmark may satisfy the auditor or your company's compliance requirement for something like PCI to allow you to process credit cards. But being compliant has nothing to do with being secure. Are you going to be *actively secure* or *passively compliant*? That's the fundamental question. Most firms try to be compliant as much as they can and believe that they are more secure if they achieve their compliance. But it just doesn't work that way because security is all encompassing and compliance really isn't."

"Okay, I get it, Jonathan. But I'm even more worried about *passing* the audits in the first place, not just how many of them there are. Remember, I'm not a security guy."

"That's why the security tools need to be thought out in order to work. There are several challenges. The first is making sure the tools are set up properly. Large and medium sized companies like Orion—also, Target was one of them—assume all the time that because they bought a high-end tool like FireEye and it's up and running on their network they must be more secure. What most of the vendors sell is what they call 'smart start,' a quick way to get the tool up and running. They extol the virtues of having that tool up and running in less than an hour like they're the cable companies."

"Yes, I've been cold called by several of those vendors since I took over this job, making that kind of promise," Tim said.

"From a simple, generic perspective you can have that," Jonathan continued. "You can plug it into the network and then watch traffic go through it, so it's up and running. But what is it actually doing? What value is it actually contributing after that first hour of existence? Security tools are very rarely set up properly or managed properly on an ongoing basis.

"There are actually two sides to managing a security tool. First is the plumbing. Just like operating systems have updates, security tools have updates. So are those updates being applied to the security tool? Are the features and functions all up to date and running the latest and greatest? And then are the rules set up properly? Are they doing what they're supposed to be doing?

"Mostly what happens with a tool like a FireEye is people put in log monitoring, FireEye sends its logs to the tool and it generates lots of alerts. It sees everything and alerts to everything. And in the case of a large retailer or some other kind of company with customers to worry about, they just start to ignore what the tool is seeing because they come to think of it all as regular behavior, what they should be seeing that on their network. They figure the tool is crying wolf, and they ignore the alerts, even when it's telling them about legitimate attacks on their networks and systems."

"Well then what should the security people focus on?" Tim asked.

"What they need is the training to answer what I call the Three Questions:

1. **What is it?**
2. **What impact is it having?**
3. **What are we going to do to fix it?**

"All the alerts are another reason I can't stand the security products like the one we use from Securesoc," Tim said. "They get installed and then all of a sudden things are popping up all the time warning me about issues. None of it seems to matter."

"If it's really a false positive," Jonathan continued, "you need to let the person in charge of maintaining the tool know so they they're not in this situation where the tool is crying wolf all the time and getting ignored. Because at some point a legitimate alert is going to come through the security tool and it's going to be ignored. That's one of the problems that occurred with Target when they were breached. The tool actually worked against them. A false sense of security can lull any company to sleep and desensitize both the client and the security company responsible for monitoring to the importance of the events unfolding before them."

Tim followed up, "In my previous companies we implemented a rule that employees are not allowed to surf inappropriate websites. The network and operations people like me monitored all the web traffic and human resources spread the message about the policy. Senior management was happy because they warded off anyone from going to gambling sites, downloading pornography, etc."

"Exactly," Jonathan said. "But if they don't have a firewall in place that actually stops their users from going to these websites, it's really just a paper policy, with nothing in place to enforce the rule, and nothing in place to monitor users' compliance to the rule. It's the same thing with many security tools: one of their biggest features may be the ability to block inappropriate activity on the network. But if that isn't turned on and the tool is left in monitor mode only, it's seeing bad things and saying, 'Well, if I was allowed to I'd stop this right now but I'm not allowed to so I'm just telling you about it instead.' It's not unusual to set up the tool like this in monitor mode to see initial traffic as part of the setup process. But the danger is leaving it in monitor mode and not dealing with the threats that come in like the tool is built to do."

"So we've got to calibrate the security tools," Tim affirmed as he pulled into the Orion parking garage.

"And the SDLC, standard imaging, network architecture...auditing," Jonathan responded.

"Right," Tim responded, embarrassed to have minimized the rest of Jonathan's diagnosis. "Okay then, let's go find the information security guy."

FRIDAY, 4:48 P.M.

Tim led Jonathan through the front doors and down a stairwell where the IT department worked. Tim's office was on the first floor, designated for the C-suite executives and their support staff. Accountants, marketing people, and human resources were upstairs. The fact that IT was relegated to the basement—the company called it the "terrace level"—symbolized its status within the organization.

When they found Jake Peters, the Director of Information Security, Tim introduced Jonathan and got an update on business operations.

"Securesoc said it would be fine to continue running customer credit cards through our traditional point of sale system, since that's a completely separate application," Jake said. "They asked for the source code to Millennial to look for vulnerabilities but Scott wouldn't give it to them."

"You talked to Securesoc?" Tim asked. His title may have made him the person in charge of Orion's relationship with its managed service security vendor, but Jake projected so little authority that Tim couldn't image him being in the loop in this basic way.

"Well, Ewan did, but it was over speakerphone and I was in the room."

"Okay—and what is Ewan doing?"

"Still trying to keep Scott from going through his operations logs."

"Of course." There was nothing Tim could do about this melee now until he plugged Jonathan in to talk with each of them one by one. All that mattered for now was that the app was shut down and he hadn't heard from Tina or anyone else upstairs in the press department about publicity—no news was good news.

Tim motioned over to the conference room, saying they wanted to run through a blueprint for a new way of doing things. Jake was surprisingly willing to go along, but Jonathan stopped Tim before he could walk any further with them into the room.

"Hold up, partner. Let Jake and I have a little one-on-one time first."

The impetus to talk to Jake solo surprised Tim. But he didn't know his own security guy that well, and maybe it would mean more to Jake if his boss weren't in there putting him on the defensive and implying that somehow this current breach was all his fault. Jake hadn't made much of an impression at all on Tim in his short time observing him at Orion. Everyone seemed to walk all over him, even the two underlings on staff working for him. In the run-up to the application's launch, he had signed off on *StrengthenPass* being the product added on at the last minute to supposedly provide improved password protection, but Tim had heard this was a move precipitated by Scott over in development, not Jake. *StrengthenPass* was the kind of bolt-on tool favored by developers who wanted to get it done to make both deadline and budget. How could any security expert worth his salt let this fly? Tim nodded and pulled up a chair, opened his laptop and started to scan his email for the latest updates on the breach.

For the next 45 minutes, Tim could hear their voices rising in competition with each other. Jake seemed like a reticent guy but it sounded like he was giving as good as he got with Jonathan. Tim tried to focus on the logging reports that Securesoc had e-mailed him throughout the afternoon but couldn't keep his concentration with the sparring match going on behind those doors.

After a lull, the two men came outside and startled Tim by exchanging a couple of big smiles and firm handshakes.

"You gave me all I could handle," Jonathan smiled to Jake, "but I really enjoyed our discussion. To be honest, I didn't expect some of the resistance you gave me, and I do this kind of thing for a living. I'm really glad we could hammer out an understanding."

Tim wondered what the hell was going on. He half expected Jake to quit after being read a version of the riot act that Jonathan had given him in the car, given that Jake was nominally in charge of everything Jonathan had outlined that was screwed up with their security. But it seemed Jake had come to terms with the consultant. Somehow they had forged a pact.

"So we're good?" was all Tim could come up with. Jonathan smiled and led him away from Jake's cubicle.

"C'mon, take me to where we can get a cup of coffee."

Sitting on benches in Orion's canteen, Jonathan walked Tim through the showdown he just had with Jake.

"Jake is like most security guys I meet with," he started. "They're caught between the actual company's demands on one end and the managed security provider's limitations and defects on the other. So on Orion's end, you have a culture that's pretty adverse to security, right? Your mission is fulfilling customer orders each day and marketing the good food and beer to new customers. Everything is directly or tangentially related to that—just as it would be toward the mission of a consulting firm or an automotive parts supplier or whatever. All these services and products require applications, but no one wants to stop and make sure those applications are secure. They just pawn that off on the security provider and check the box."

So at Orion, just like most companies, the security guy is actually *powerless*. His interest is something that the rest of the company doesn't care about, and they've contracted out to Securesoc instead of listening to him. We can gripe about Jake's lackluster performance leading into today all we want, but it was really the logical outcome of the role carved out for him in a do-nothing role here at Orion. He was likely just hired to check another box."

All of a sudden Tim felt sympathy for Jake replacing his frustration. If Jonathan was right, he wasn't a fall guy in the collapse of Millennial like he'd originally envisioned, rather Jake was just another casualty of the way Orion treated IT, and security in particular.

"What does Jake want then?" Tim asked. "What was with him raising his voice repeatedly in there? I guess it was the culture here that made him powerless, not his own personality like I had always assumed."

"He let it all off his chest about being neglected here. He started by claiming that the SDLC and the standard imaging protocols were working just fine. He did everything he was tasked with doing. That was just Jake trying to cover his ass though. Once he realized that I wasn't here to fire him, he admitted that security was just an afterthought in the development process, and that the tools the company had at its disposal through Securesoc were being used to avoid any interference with operations, not actual intrusion prevention. I asked Jake what he does all day to pretend like he matters here, and he said basically he does what the developers and operations people ask him to do. That was the only way he could garner some respect for his little fiefdom—by pretending he was an essential player even though security has been practically nonexistent.

"That's how the Millennial mess happened. Jake told me that before you were hired as CIO, the developers approached him and got him to sign off on their SDLC. Guess where security was? Static testing at the end, but before it went online. So they did a quick check to make sure there was no horribly bad code, then went live with the thing without testing, probably to make your company's arbitrary bullshit deadline."

Tim pictured the developers intimidating Jake into this arrangement. No wonder they shipped Millennial on time—by cutting corners wherever they could. They turned Jake into their accomplice, and as a side benefit likely set him up as a scapegoat so that in the event things went wrong, they figured Jake could be the fall guy.

"So then I painted the picture that I did for you in the car," Jonathan explained. "I ran through what it would look like when the testing is done right, the images are updated whenever the patching is done, and the tools are calibrated to stop intrusions rather than be ignored. Jake bought into all this but still didn't think he'd have the authority to execute it. He seemed really afraid of the bureaucratic structure you've got here. I leveled with Jake and told him he has two options: try becoming empowered here as the person responsible for security and help get it done right with help from you and me, or go somewhere else and be treated like a lapdog again. He said he would try option one. That's how we finished with a meetings of the minds."

"Well you got more out of Jake in 45 minutes than I have in two weeks," Tim admitted. He was happy that at least one of his employees was now empowered to do his job the right way. Tim thought about the transformation in his role that Jake would need to make: going from a lackey to a watchdog. But if Jake could see that he had the running room to secure Orion's applications and systems, then he had every incentive to do his job well. For the first time, Jake would get to feel and act like information security mattered, rather than being treated as an afterthought or an annoyance to work around.

After they finished their cups of coffee Tim and Jonathan decided to hunt down the operations manager, Ewan Watt. Tim hoped Ewan could tell them specifically what was impacting Millennial from the information contained in those logs he wouldn't let the developers see, tell them what he knew was happening in the app before it got shut down, and what changes were needed to prevent such a catastrophe from happening again. Tim's crusade of using Jonathan to simultaneously put out fires and help identify ways to restructure the IT department was moving forward. He took a hint of satisfaction already in starting to prove Jeff's assumptions wrong.

"Wait, go get him first," Jonathan said.

"Who?" Tim asked.

"Jake! He's part of the team now."

FRIDAY, 6:02 P.M.

After bringing Jake into the fold, the three headed down the long hallway across the terrace level to Orion's IT operations center, managed by Ewan Grant.

Ewan was a Scotsman, plucked from the same role at a rival fast casual restaurant company. Tim suspected that Orion had chosen Ewan because it was a safe pick: he'd already run IT operations at a similar-sized business in the same industry, so no one could say he wasn't qualified. The problem was that it appeared that Ewan *wasn't* qualified. Routine tasks like patching and hardware replacement seemed to be mired with difficulty. Employees upstairs in finance and marketing seemed to hang on to their old laptops rather then turn them in for the upgrades Orion purchased, finding the convoluted process to swap to a new machine not worth the hassle.

The first couple days on the job, Tim made an effort to chat up various desk workers at headquarters over lunch and coffee to see what their experiences with IT at the company were like. He learned that most of the accountants were working on dated versions of their software systems, even though they didn't seem to know it. Some of the creative people brought their own Mac notebooks to work because they needed the graphic design functions. Problems like these were fairly mundane, and Tim had tried to shove them out of his head for the time being due to the Millennial rollout. But they nagged at him as a harbinger that things were far from smooth in operations.

Jonathan cordoned off the conference room the same way he had done earlier, but this time invited Tim and Jake to join him around the table with Ewan. Several designates from Securesoc had come into Orion to sift through the breach, and were huddled around a row of computers with Ewan's people. Tim thought it was a good sign that the security provider finally seemed to be taking a more hands-on approach compared to that morning. Maybe Ewan would be able to tell them something.

"So what do we know?" Jonathan barked. Secretly, Tim was relieved that Jonathan could play the bad cop when he needed to this way. It spared him from being the bad guy while fresh on the scene as the boss.

"We've gotten real-time reports all day from the folks here with Securesoc. I've also been in touch with the FBI agents assigned to the case that Tim authorized me to talk with. The initial estimate on number of compromised users' credit card data and personal information has held up."

"No, no, no. That's not what I'm asking," Jonathan shot back. "I want to know, where did the initial leak occur? What was the weakness that was in our system that allowed a bad guy to get in?"

Silence fell over the conference table. Ewan squirmed in his seat. "Well, Securesoc still isn't sure about that, and of course the developers don't have a..."

Jonathan cut in. "You have no idea. I could tell from your facial response. It's actually okay. I mean, it's not really okay. It's disappointing. But it doesn't matter as much now. The app wasn't ready to go live and should never have been launched. I'm not here to fix the app. You've shut Millennial down, which seems to be the only thing anyone here did right this morning, and at this point we're not here to fix it. What I am here to do it is trace how exactly this happened, so it doesn't keep happening to you. We're going to make some significant changes to the way things are being done in your department. Got it?"

Ewan swallowed and nodded simultaneously. The good news was his shoulders were no longer slumped in the chair. Jonathan's energized approach had taken away all lethargy, and he and Jake were both at attention.

"I had a conversation with Jake earlier, and we talked about how to make information security matter again at this company. I wouldn't have this meeting without Jake here because operations are the other side of the coin, especially for tools—which are the beating heart of security. If they are not working the way they're supposed to then we're porous. So let's talk about what I call the *Operations Conundrum*...

"What is 'operations' anyway? It's people—that's what it means. It's all sorts of questions about people. The first as it relates to the mess Orion is in, is who is going to run the security tools? In most companies where security is approached passively, there's someone who's responsible for security, but he has no control and he's not empowered to do anything. That's Jake over here—at least until this afternoon.

"So since Jake has been emasculated here's what I see has happened. Securesoc was handed off to Ewan and his operations team, who are managing the routers, the switches, the servers, and everything else. What happens is they managed that service and the security tools the same way they managed the network switch. They thought about it as another network device on the network. They didn't understand security, because they're operations people, not security people.

"The alerts from things may have gone to a Jake who has to do investigations, but he can't actually effect any changes on the network at all. And so traditionally, those devices, in most companies, the tools like firewalls are not treated like the security devices that they are and they don't get the respect or the attention to do the job you're purchasing them for. That looks like what's happened here. Securesoc was handed to the operations group to work with instead of going to a security group to interface with them from a security perspective. It's a matter of perspective and priority. Does the company treat security as its own sphere of influence or as an add-on responsibility of operations?

"I'm not asking that as a rhetorical question. I want one of you guys to answer me."

Jake spoke up. "It's been treated as an after-thought. My title is Information Security Director, but I have spent most of my time putting out little fires for people, not working with Securesoc and making sure it functions properly."

Tim was startled by Jake speaking up in front of Ewan like this. Just like inside the other conference room with Jonathan, he was getting the bureaucratic dysfunction of Orion's IT department off of his chest.

"Okay," Jonathan continued. "Let's continue to draw out the implications of this. It means that the plumbing being done by the operations team is more the type of plumbing they would do on a router or on a switch. The approach there is, 'Okay, Cisco just released a new version of the switch software, I'll apply that. Okay, the vendor of our firewall just released a new version of the software, let's have Securesoc install it.' To be fair to Ewan and his staff, they aren't oriented to thinking about tuning the actual rules that are on there. In their minds, they can plug the tool into the network and make sure it's running the latest operating system and then they're done. That's the scope of managing the device to them.

Ewan actually nodded.

Jonathan went on: "At the end of the day, information security people appear to be in a position of responsibility, but they have no authority to go along with that responsibility.

So they're responsible for keeping our systems secure, they're responsible for building policies, or they're responsible for making sure you're not doing things you're not supposed to be doing, but they have no authority whatsoever. It's a real challenge. That's why I get most of the consulting calls I get.

"The security principals like Jake are usually stuck in the middle because they're the first person who gets called if there's a breach, and they're the ones the company is going to yell at and demand answers from. Didn't you want to do that when we first got here this afternoon, Tim? But Jake had no role in the tools that Orion bought or their management. Yet somehow he's responsible for security because that's in his title.

"The challenge in finding out where the breach actually originated from is that a lot of times the operations team doesn't really know what the application is doing. So the development team is giving the operations team a finished application, saying install this or update it, but they're not really cognizant of how the application works. There are all sorts of subsets of data among different servers. So it's very difficult for them to say where the breach might be coming from. They could say, 'Well, it's one of these 12 servers because that's our application farm, but beyond that, we don't know.'"

Ewan spoke up now: "That's exactly what our situation is. We have no idea how Millennial was supposed to work. We went over wireframes with the development team in the beginning and then had a walkthrough of the finished product right before it shipped. Everything in between—no idea. We didn't know how it was built so we have no idea where the information could be leaking from and ending up in the attackers' hands."

"Yes—that's what I thought," answered Jonathan. "Now it looks like you're focused on protecting Team Operations, which is likely why you brought Securesoc here to your side of the building to perform their investigation.

"But that actually slows things down because instead of having a team of people that are all looking into the breach, where one person may notice something that somebody else might miss, the focus seems to be on minimizing the impact of operations involvement, or lack thereof, to preventing the breach. At this point, we don't even know if the breach could have originated from inside the company, heck it could be one of Orion's employees who's the source of the leak.

"Here's the thing," Jonathan continued. "If Orion doesn't have proper controls and can't eliminate its own people as being a source of the problem up front that adds significantly to the overall investigation and the process of plugging the breach. Because if you have to spend your time investigating everything it takes you a lot longer to find what the root cause is and then be able to shut it down. Isolating the problem up front is the best head start you can ask for.

"Besides putting his team in place and making assignments for each area—operations, network, and security—the biggest question a CIO like Tim faces in response to the breach is when and how to shut down the business systems. Well,

Millennial is already shut down. But I bet Orion doesn't even have a business continuity plan. Tim, am I right?"

Tim gulped. Now he was on the spot. It was true: in the two weeks of squeezing inside the company and trying to get a handle on how the app was going to ship, Tim hadn't even contemplated the idea of building any type of BCP, and didn't know if anything already existed.

"You're right, Jonathan. We don't have a BCP. It's my responsibility."

"Well, let's talk about why you have a BCP in the first place, so we understand how it might have helped with the current breach," Jonathan answered firmly. "Since it's a business decision on top of a security one it affects different aspects of the business. Is Orion willing to be down for a period of time if something else gets breached? If it's going to cost so many thousands of dollars per hour, how long is your company willing to be down for? I mean, if the traditional point of sale system—not just the mobile app—is hacked, do you stop serving lunch to your customers right now?

"Consider the risks that go through your C-level executives' minds, especially the CEO. If they make the decision to shut something down and there is significant profit impact from that decision, critics among the shareholders once they go public and in the media can say after the fact that they shouldn't have shut down. So the decision-maker is left taking the heat instead of being rewarded or recognized for resolving the security problem.

"I can't tell you how many times I've been parachuted in to a company where somebody made a decision and said, 'I'm willing to take a risk of exposing more information until we shut this thing down properly.' And that risk, for sure, exposed more information. Whether it was 10 percent more or 90 percent more, more information was exposed based on a decision not to shut the system down. Anyone remember a little company called Target, for instance? Even when they were informed about the breach, they spent three days trying to decide on a response, resulting in millions more customers being affected.

"For consumer-facing firms like you guys in the burger and fries business, it's usually a choice that hinges on customer inconvenience. A company doesn't want to close its doors even for a few hours. It doesn't want to have to do credit card transactions by hand. So it hums along on the sales end like nothing's happened, while the breach continues and the information leakage gets worse.

"But there's more at stake than that, of course. It comes down to egg on their face versus reputational risk. Closing down or bringing in those manual credit card machines might look amateurish, but they're a fair price to pay for stopping the exposure of information into the wild. *Overreacting to the emergency is better than underreacting*. You'll earn your customers' respect and may even save your reputation. Of course speed really is of the essence when responding, time is your enemy in these situations."

"Consider the case of Tylenol in the 1980s when it pulled its capsules off the shelves overnight in response to a suspected poisonous tampering. Their handling of that crisis became a legend for them because it revealed how much they care about their customers. Stopping one Tylenol customer from dying was more important than anything else!

"Remember, setting up a new policy like a BCP cannot just happen with the snap of your fingers. It may mean deciding, how are you communicating this out to the stores? How are you letting each store know that they need to do this? How are you letting the public know? Do you have signs that are printed and they're in the back and all the signs are ready to go, and you just pull them out and we put one on each cash register to let them know? Or you put them on the front door and just say 'unable to process credit card transactions electronically, so there may be a longer than usual wait at the cash register.' Crap like that matters in executing your BCP. You have to plan it all ahead of time."

Jonathan's emphasis on the BCP sparked the first serious discussion Tim realized he had been engaged in at Orion with his IT staff in his two weeks there. Jake and Ewan were obviously scared by the day's experience so far and wanted to make sure it never happened again. They were also coming out of their shells and realizing the blame (and the responsibility) that fell to themselves and to others. For the next thirty minutes they talked about having a plan in place for handling IT operations during a breach. This included shutting the systems down, when they should disconnect everything from the Internet, disconnect from the network, and bringing the systems back online but isolated so they could be tested before being plugged into anything. They broke down how Ewan would make a copy of everything and Jake would be the one to inspect it before it went live again.

They talked about contingencies Jonathan introduced, such as if they ever had to go to court—certainly a plausible scenario with Millennial after today, as Daniel from Securesoc had hinted at that morning. Everything needed to be preserved as evidence in a certain way, to demonstrate a proper chain of custody. It needed to show that Orion had a very solid process that they were following, so that there would be no way that any of those compromised forensic information collected could get contaminated with data from something else, or they weren't infected before but now they got infected after they turned them back on. It would be due diligence in protecting the company from further economic damage in sorting out the breach after it was identified and shut down.

Just as the two seemed to be getting along, Jonathan reintroduced tension again. He seemed like a specialist at this, pushing and pulling the emotions of the otherwise introverted information technicians.

"It's important to not let the security versus operations tension get lost in the shuffle. Let's admit it: Jake and Ewan, you guys kind of resent each other. But that's actually normal. Our job is to make this relationship functional. Remember, security is not typically part of operations. At some firms, they don't even want to be in the same room together, at the same meetings. Be prepared for a struggle when holding your planning meeting about security, to get Ewan's operation's team's buy-in to work together with Jake's information security team. They don't consider the topic to be in their wheelhouse because they are focused on operations, not disaster preparation. And Tim, it's your job from here on out to be the arbitrator, the neutral broker; the role I've been playing here today.

"The tension cuts both ways. The security folks don't typically consider themselves to be part of the operations team. They're picturing themselves in a different situation than the guys that are day-to-day operations. And a lot of them have come from that—and they enjoy where they are now. Jake, where did you come up from in the IT world?"

"Well, I was a network administrator before making the jump to security," Jake answered. "I just really liked the security aspect of IT and at my last company made the leap to it full-time. I was happy to leave operations behind."

"Okay," Jonathan continued. "That's what I was going to guess—network administrator. So you worked your way out of that to get into security because you really liked it. You understood that world but got yourself out of it."

Jake beamed, but Jonathan wasn't trying to build him up.

"So instead of embracing it and using the knowledge that you have of that world, you adopted a different attitude: 'I did that in the past, I don't want to do that anymore, so I don't want to get involved in that,' or 'I don't even want to think about that.' And so you and other security guys look at operations as being almost beneath you, something that was on your career path, and is now in the rearview. Because otherwise you would have proactively gotten involved with Ewan's side of the building."

Jonathan turned away from Jake's souring expression toward Tim.

"It's one of the CIO's greatest challenges to get these two sides to work together, both in preventing a security breach and fixing one that's happened. The best way for you to do that is to take the vision of the company and then make IT meet that vision by seeing where they fit in. It's understanding the company's vision and getting your team to respond and to work together to be able to deliver on that vision. That's really what you're supposed to be doing.

"Tim, what kind of have a relationship do you have with your CEO?

Tim wasn't sure how to answer this in front of two people under him on the org chart. In the spirit of the day he decided to be candid.

"Well, I'd say Jeff and I have some relationship building to do. I respect him but he kind of treats IT like a distraction. He told me he wanted someone good to run it when he hired me, but his attitude was that he wanted to just get that out of the way so IT would be invisible."

"Exactly!" Jonathan followed up. "It's often a challenge for the CIO to communicate to his boss that he needs resources to make IT more a part of the company's vision. This is where consultants like me are often brought in because even though the CIO is saying it, the CEO needs to hear it from an outside voice. It's the old notion that exists across any division, whether it's finance or marketing or IT. C-level executives and budget setters are always wary of a division leader trying to get more money, more people, just more in general. The CIO is legitimately trying to help the business but there's always that question of, 'where is this coming from? What's Tim getting all worked up about?'

"So Jeff needs assurance and validation. If you've got a really good group of C-level executives working together and they trust each other and work closely to solve problems, that doesn't arise nearly as much. But with as cyclical as employment is these days, even at the top level where Fortune 500 CEOs are replaced every three to five years on average, it's difficult to build that kind of trust.

"Tim—I know you've been here two weeks; how long as Jeff been here?"

"Eighteen months," Tim replied.

"There you go. Same thing probably applies for the rest of his executives. Tim, do you realize what that means? You are in a sales job. You have to be telling Jeff that the things you and Jake and Ewan want will deliver a return on investment. You've got to match the firm's goals—whether it's 20 percent more revenue or a certain number of total transactions—and pitch the resources you'll need to enable Orion to execute those topline goals.

“Now, this always comes with pushback. ‘Well, we’re already able to do this, why can’t we just get by without it...?’ or ‘Can’t we just muddle along with what we have right now until we need that more?’ The CIO is trying to plan for that growth, but the CEO wants the growth to happen first before spending real money on supporting it. There’s always this push-pull dynamic between IT and the rest of the corporate hierarchy, just like there’s that push-pull in IT itself between you guys in operations and security.”

Sony has really opened a lot of corporate leaders’ eyes about the urgency of upgrading security. It’s not that Sony was hacked once; they got hacked in waves. Operation centers in Asia, Australia and North America were all hacked. But the one that really brought it home for everybody was the breach in late 2014, purported to originate from North Korea in response to the movie, “The Interview.” Right before it was scheduled to premiere, the hackers got into Sony’s upcoming movies and email communications. The head of Sony Pictures Entertainment was promptly fired after derogatory comments she made about Barack Obama and Angelina Jolie, among others, were leaked in the hack.

They were obviously pretty confident it was

the North Korean regime that was driving it. But there was a significant insider component to it where somebody on the inside had to have collaborated, because by the way happened there was just far too much access for it to have been done completely from the outside.

That really forced a lot of companies to look at their own operations, which up to that point, they hadn't. That significant event forced other similar sized firms to get their houses in order to they don't become another Target or Sony. It was a major scare to global companies across all industries.

For its part, Sony hadn't learned from its mistakes because it was breached four years prior through its PlayStation network when 110 million credentials were stolen. The PlayStation network was taken down entirely for approximately three days around Christmas, when a lot of people got their new PlayStations as gifts, plugged them in and booted them up, and couldn't use them because they couldn't get on the network.

It's one thing for a breach like this to happen once or even twice to an organization like Sony, but consumers did not have a lot of sympathy for them when they were attacked most recently (even if it was from North Korea) because it was the latest in a long line of attacks. It was clear for all to see that Sony hadn't learned from its mistakes and left itself porous.

The upside for similar-sized companies is that they're opening their eyes in a big way where they thought before they had "good enough" security and it's forcing them to reconsider. Sony obviously did make changes after the breaches happened, and yet they still got breached again. So the firms that haven't been breached and also haven't made any changes, what's their level of susceptibility? What are they exposed to? They are on a track to become the next Sonys and Targets of the world.

What is it? What's the impact? What are we supposed to do about it? Tim thought of Jonathan's Three Questions raised in the car. They were important for the executives upstairs to understand about today's attack, but also for the IT department itself to understand. Tim wasn't sure they had sunk in.

"Jonathan, the Securesoc team has been looking through the logs all day, trying to figure out what happened this morning with Millennial. Obviously, that doesn't work as a security prevention measure. We can't have people manually looking through the logs all the time. So what are we supposed to do to head this off again from a security-operations point of view?"

"Automation, automation, automation!" Jonathan boomed. "You need to be looking for threats all the time, and you can't do that manually. Use logging tools to monitor points of vulnerability. The most important things to monitor give you visibility into the operating systems, visibility into the performance of the systems themselves, and visibility into the applications. If you had been monitoring that visibility into the Millennial application you might have stopped the attack before it started."

"That's what Scott over in development wants to do—go through the logs manually," Ewan interjected. "It's his way of confusing the issue from the crappy code he deployed by messing with operations' tools."

"I'll deal with him later," Jonathan shot back, having no patience for squabbling with someone who wasn't even in the room. "Right now I think *you're* trying to confuse the issue. What about automation then? You know what might be one of the most effective things to automate? Testing. Testing is what lets you know if the application works and if it's secure before it ships to your customers. The automation makes sure you actually do the testing, instead of relying on human interaction to make sure it gets done. There should be an assembly line of tests that the application goes through as it moves down the line in production. Think of the brilliant Toyota assembly line—the testing you do should reflect the same rigor and discipline."

"Right now I do the testing we have going on with our apps and also the patching," Ewan said. "My team is configured to take on those things. I know it has to work better, but I don't think that means all of a sudden it should switch over to Jake down the hall. He doesn't have experience leading a team through these things, even if they are security-related."

Tim couldn't believe Ewan's attempts to keep control of this aspect, but reminded himself that was a fact of life in the IT world—managers defending their turf, trying to protect and preserve every bit of power they felt they had fought so hard to attain. It was about job security, their loyalty to their own teams, but at its core it was also about ego. Ewan didn't want to humble himself to let Scott or Jake into the zone of responsibility, even though Jake was the security expert.

"I'll give you some good reasons why," Jonathan stated in response. "Because it's the thing that's going to save you. Either you're going to integrate with security and make yourself into an assembly line of testing, and make sure that patching is completed thoroughly each time with new standard images, or you and your team are going to continue to botch things here.

"It's not about your capabilities," Jonathan continued. "Basic functions of security like testing and patching aren't supposed to be done just inside operations. They need the focus and attention to detail on security from the guy who actually spends all of his time thinking about it, not the operations manager who has other issues like functionality to worry about. When the application loads a little but slower, do you and the developers want to be the ones who answer to your CEO about that or do you want it to be Jake, the guy who can actually explain the necessity of that extra half second due to the presence of a firewall?

"The security director is the one who can provide the intellectual defense of these tools and procedures that you just can't do because you're biased toward operations. So you need to accept the limitations of your role but know that on the flipside you'll be better at your job and less likely to have egg on your face the way you do today."

"Okay, I see your point," Ewan responded. "I can work with Jake if he'll meet me halfway. I've actually always wanted my department to work in a more regimented manner and be integrated with the rest of IT at Orion. Considering we're the nerve center of IT we feel really isolated. And I don't want another situation like what happened with Millennial where we're the first targets. But that still leaves the guys in development led by Scott who program our applications without regard for testing or consideration of really any security at all. How am I supposed to be on top of it when they basically sabotage me like they've done with Millennial?"

"Oh, I've got a plan for them, too," Jonathan exclaimed, almost giddily.

SATURDAY, 8:18 A.M.

After getting Ewan's buy-in, Tim and Jonathan checked in with the Securesoc team onsite as they were continuing to go through the logs line-by-line. Jonathan left for his hotel while Tim ordered pizza and stayed to support the group efforts to further try to isolate the source of the breach. It was becoming clear they weren't going to pinpoint where the breach occurred. It was like looking for a needle in a haystack.

Before he left around midnight, Tim issued an ultimatum: "Barring any new findings, we're going to rebuild the Millennial application server early tomorrow morning. I'll tell Glenn."

As the network/systems administrator, Glenn was in charge of the client-server architecture and responsible for executing tasks like web, mail, printing, remote file access, proprietary applications and databases that connected through Orion's network to the servers assigned to support each function. If Ewan and the operations team were engaged in the plumbing of IT, and responsible for the network and systems, Glenn had the 50,000-foot view because he ran these big dedicated systems.

To Tim, that explained why Glenn was by far the snidest, most arrogant manager in Orion's IT department. He had dominion over the basic relationship of each IT core operation between an application, a server and its clients. He had been at Orion longer than anyone in IT, and this tenure had enabled him to build a protective moat around his role. Most people thought of Glenn as the guy with the keys to the kingdom: if anything were to happen to Glenn, many people thought that Orion's IT systems would implode.

For these reasons, Tim was reluctant to tell Glenn himself that he was going to need him to deploy a new server, so he brought Jake and Ewan along to explain the approach from a security and operations perspective. Before they began the walk over to Glenn's office to bring explain the plan, Tim called Jonathan to let him know what he was doing.

"Just hold on, I'm almost back at your office. I want to talk with you, Jake and your network/systems guy about this. There are a number of pitfalls in making the move."

Perplexed, Tim hung up the phone and waited for Jonathan. What does he want to warn us about, he wondered. Replacing the server was basically their safest card to play, and it seemed like a no-brainer.

"I know, I know, I know," Jonathan practically yelled at he

walked down the hall toward Tim's office. "You want to replace the server. It's a gut instinct and it feels holistic and dramatic. I get that. But it's too good to be true."

"What do you mean?" Tim asked.

"The problem is if the replacement server image hasn't been updated continuously—the problem we talked about in the car ride over here yesterday—the weaknesses that are on the old server image will migrate to the new one. You think it's going to solve the problem but it ends up putting the exact same weakness that was there in the first place in the operating system back on the network. Then the attack repeats itself. Not what you guys want to happen."

"Okay, I get it," Tim replied, annoyed at himself for blanking on the gold image challenge they had discussed on the way back from the airport. He was now running on fumes from the adrenaline of yesterday's events, and his brain was a little foggy. Jonathan on the other hand seemed to be enlivened on the second day of his consultancy here.

"Let's all go see Glenn, the network/systems guy, and figure out what we're going to do and how he can help us."

Glenn's workspace was on the same terrace level of the rest of the IT department, but in a far corner facing away from the courtyard that seemed to prohibit much light or activity from entering. His office had the most personalization of anyone's Tim had seen at Orion, including Jeff's, thanks to his having been at the company for six out its eight years of existence. Glenn even had an "ego wall" of pictures of himself with industry-related celebrities, much like a CEO would have. What a prima donna, Tim thought.

"Our plan has been to replace the server," Tim started. "But..."

Before he could get any further Glenn interrupted him.

"Did that late last night, after everyone left. My team has actually tested Millennial offline this morning with some of the developers, and it appears to be functioning properly again. No obvious holes or operational meltdown like we encountered yesterday. No evidence of information leaking out. I'd recommend some further testing the rest of the weekend here and then a re-launch of the app when the stores open for lunch on Monday if it continues to pass the tests. The media probably won't even bother covering the hack if it's taken care of over the weekend."

Tim was livid at Glenn for replacing the server on his own and for going around Ewan's back to do testing with the developers. And for presuming to craft a public relations strategy while he was at it. He was about to launch into his first bona fide tirade as the new IT boss at Orion before Jonathan jumped in.

"Let me stop you there because that path is headed for catastrophe. The original server is gone but the hole that allowed the hackers in is almost certainly still there. Yeah, you put the new server back online and the application seems to be working fine since late last night. But I guarantee you before Monday morning the exact same behavior will happen again because you put the exact same vulnerability back on the network and so the same way the bad guys got in last time still exists, so they can come back in again. Or even worse, they WON'T compromise the system right away, giving us a false sense of security that we've fixed the problem, let us go live again on Monday, start collecting even more customer information, and then they'll break back in using the same method and the problem will start all over again. But it will be even worse next time, because we'll basically have to acknowledge that we knew there was a problem and did nothing to prevent it from happening again."

Glenn's face looked nonplussed.

"Even though you've removed the system that was compromised, because it was all blown away and rebuilt from scratch the original vulnerability they used to get in is likely still there so the intruders can use that same attack vector and get right back in at a time of their choosing. So believe me, replacing the server is not going to solve your problem today. You'd be setting Orion up for round two on Monday. Not that I thought Tim would okay that." Jonathan glanced at Tim with a sly grin. "We have some indication that the breach point may be a 3rd party application. Until we remove it from the Millennial app entirely and then do further security testing there's no way this app will be ready to go back online."

"How are the intruders so effective?" Tim asked.

"These back-to-back break-ins happen all the time. The hackers have likely found an easy back door and they've taken advantage of it. They typically go for the low hanging fruit first so they're not spending a lot of time crafting a really custom exploit that would only work in a special environment. They have access and then suddenly it stops working. One of the first things they'll do is go back and see if that same thing that they used last time and exploited still exists. 'Is it still there? Yes. There it is. Okay. I'll go ahead and do it again.' And then they pick up right where they left off, at a time of their choosing."

Jonathan then ran through multiple ways this could have been prevented during the server replacement. If the systems team does a vulnerability assessment against every new server before they actually make it live on the network, they could find the vulnerability and then patch it themselves. Even better, they test the server for operating system and network vulnerabilities first, and then test the application once it's deployed for application specific vulnerabilities. But that usually doesn't happen because they are not working in concert with the security team that would instruct them to do the vulnerability scan in the first place. Sure enough, Jake had been left out of the picture too.

Glenn and Jake were both smart people, Tim conceded. But they weren't relying on each other or using each other's assistance to work together to effectively solve this problem. Glenn was doing his own thing with the server as an ad hoc solution to make the problem go away rather than coming up with a comprehensive approach to resolution. They'd actually be far better taking off taking the server offline to do the security scan.

Instead Glenn was thinking, "Let's just get the damn thing up and running because the customers are impacted!" He probably had a direct line to Jeff or one of the C-level folks on this one, given that he had so much institutional knowledge and connections at the company. Of course, Orion didn't have a business continuity plan in place so it wasn't executing one. That enabled Glenn to roll the server out and go back to the last good version of it, and he put back last week's version of it and assumed that would just solve the problem on Monday morning.

To be fair, Jake didn't know any more than these guys did about the problem, or what caused the problem. He knew that the applications server is the one that's affected, because the information that's being leaked is stored on that server. Ultimately, that was where the information resided that was compromised. He just didn't know what weakness in the system was compromised.

"Glenn, before you blew the server box away, Jake's security team should have been provided the opportunity to take an image of the box," Jonathan said. "They could have done a proper forensics investigation and tried to determine what was done in order to compromise it and then what information was actually taken from the box.

"That follow-up investigation is critical," Jonathan continued. "The response team—led by information security—may know that the problem was that server and they need to fix it but they don't know what the vulnerability was that was taken advantage of to get in. They don't know whether or not other things have been installed on that box. By taking an image and being able to deploy the image in isolation, they could look to see if the intruders installed some other type of malware. Did they put a new back door in? If so security can go back and look at all of the other systems on the entire network to see if that back door exists anywhere else because now they know what the bad guy is using in order to try to get back in later. Using that information will lead to a much better understanding of what's happening on the network. Your approach, while well-intentioned, has destroyed the forensic evidence we may need to prove where the breach came from and also to determine the full extent of what information was stolen.

Now at least Glenn started to look a little guilty.

"I mentioned Software Development Life Cycle once before," Jonathan continued. "Well there's also Server Deployment Life Cycle."

Tim knew where he was going with this. Build books and run books. A build book tells you how to build a server, stage a server, and how to deploy the applications that goes with it. And it tells you how to test it. That's all part of getting it ready for production. Whereas a run book tells you how to operate a server. It tells you what you should be doing on that server once a day, once a week, once a month, once a quarter, or by the situation. It provides a set of guidelines to actually manage or maintain the server.

"I've never used build books and run books, I've got my own checklist," Glenn retorted.

"Yes, that's what most companies do, unfortunately," Jonathan replied. When he asked to see it, Glenn said it wasn't handy.

Jonathan continued: "The best approach is what I call *attain and maintain*. You're trying to attain high levels of security, compliance, and best practices. That's what your build books will help you achieve. And once you get there, you want to make sure you're going to stay there, that's where the run book comes in. The run books are the bibles that Ewan and his operations team, along with Glenn and whoever is supporting the applications need to follow. Part of that build process for a new server should be checking to make sure the server is configured according to the build book, patches applied, unnecessary services shut down, proper auditing and logging enabled. You do those things to help reduce risk and make the systems more secure. And then ongoing we periodically check to make sure all of those things are still working as configured and expected.

"So Glenn, the systems team in charge of the servers should be coordinating with information security to compile the build and run books to make sure they are thorough. You guys are already busy running existing servers, so there's an inclination to go light on the number of steps needs for pure efficiency. But this is about security, not efficiency. One hundred steps might be necessary, but a systems person will want to put down 10 if he thinks he can get away with it.

"Don't let him do that," Jonathan said as he turned toward Jake.

Tim liked this idea of the methodical Jake being a check on

Glenn when making the build and run books. Because Glenn, as the systems/network guy, was clearly not thinking about things from a hacker's perspective who's trying to break into the box. He's thinking about the application that he's going to install. There is a list of things that he has to do to make sure that application can be supported. Then he may be thinking about it from how it's going to physically or virtually connect to the network, ensuring it is set up in a certain way because of the switch it's plugging into or because of the routes that it has to take. Security would be an afterthought for him in almost all cases. He openly acknowledged that with his idea to avoid media attention with an ill-fated Millennial re-launch.

"For the build and run books," Jonathan went on, "the information security team is able to inject all of the security related things into the process and ensure there's a complete life cycle process for the servers, from initial build through ongoing operations and ultimately when the time comes to properly decommissioning each server and system in a secure fashion.

With this in mind, and understanding how important it is to have a process when deploying new devices onto the network and then maintaining them, I think we have a better idea of how we could not just deploy a new server and re-introduce the same problems that may have led to the current breach, but instead deploy a new server that is hardened, tested to identify and fix any vulnerabilities, and then secured to prevent the same breach from occurring again. Without this approach, any activities we take, well-intentioned or otherwise, may just result in perpetuating the breach, and may even make the problem worse.

Exacerbating or extending the breach, Tim thought. The idea was somewhat startling: anyone not helping shut it down—which Tim originally thought was pretty much everyone on Orion's IT floor—was just making it worse. That showed how vital the answer was to Jonathan's third of his three questions: **What are we going to do about it?**

Tim's mind drifted to the security breaches he had encountered in his 15-year career working in the IT space. There was the hacking into the email server at the law firm he worked at right out of college. There was another time where his consulting firm's cloud-based software was infected, leaving everyone upset that the internal messaging service was down for several days. In just about every case he could remember, Tim realized, no one on his IT operations teams thought it was security related in the first place. They all assumed it was the network. They noticed the Internet slowed, and pinned it on the network. When that didn't pan out as the culprit their next suspect was the application. Always too many users on the network or too many users on the application, Tim remembered hearing. A security intrusion was almost inconceivable.

Tim brought up this past experience to Jonathan, wanting to bounce it off of a well-traveled IT consultant like him.

"That is actually quite common," Jonathan said. "Usually as the breach happens, you hear the network and systems guys saying, 'I don't even think there is a breach. I just think it's because of that new firewall I put on there. That switch there is really saturated and there's not enough traffic. I think putting in a new switch will solve the problem,' so you've got somebody who doesn't even understand what's happening who is adding to the issue by trying to fix a problem that doesn't even exist."

Tim compared Glenn with his colleagues at work in the past, those who had the same instinct to freelance troubleshoot by isolating and eliminating all the things they believed the problem could possibly stem from. Only after they had exhausted those things did they have to declare, "Oh, maybe it's a security issue."

At least Jake was trained to assume it's a security incident until proven otherwise. Tim looked at Jake, who projected an air of caution. His self-presentation versus Glenn's cockiness mirrored the way the two potential IT scenarios—security vs. operational—were so diametrically opposed.

Every security expert Tim had ever worked with wanted to focus on security and eliminating that as the source of the problem because if he doesn't eliminate that first then if it's legitimate there's more information being sucked out into the wild. Like what happened with Orion. More credit card numbers, more Social Security numbers, more customer information, whatever information the intruders got their hands on.

Whereas from the other side, the operations, network and systems people don't want to get the security guy involved because he's going to expect them to consider security and they don't think it has anything to do with security. They always had their own theory borne out of their previous experience. It was linked to whatever happened in the past, usually something as mundane as a switch or a server requiring a reboot. When they performed the reset everything started working again; problem solved. Why bother getting an inquisitive guy like Jake involved?

Tim zoned back into the conversation and realized that Jonathan had moved on and was talking about troubleshooting.

"The complication with troubleshooting is that you have people that are intuitive troubleshooters and then there are learned troubleshooters," he said. "The learned guy says, 'Well, I had this problem before and I fixed it this way,' so then when that problem happens again, the first thing he does is try to fix it the same way he did last time. If that doesn't work then he'll try other things that have worked for him in the past for other situations. Only once he's exhausted his repertoire of 'fixes' will he try to find a new way.

"The intuitive guy, on the other hand, doesn't look at what he did last time. In almost all cases he can understand what the problem is right now and he can intuitively go to what the most likely cause of the issue is. The problem is that, especially when it comes to network and systems, most employees are learned troubleshooters not intuitive troubleshooters. They don't have the background and expertise to troubleshoot intuitively."

Suddenly Jake spoke up. "I'm an intuitive troubleshooter, because I'm not someone who's always just done security. Like I told you, before this I did network and systems."

“Exactly,” Jonathan exclaimed with a finger pointed at Jake. “You’ve got that server and network operations background which allows you to overlay the information security knowledge. The result is more intuitive decisions because it’s a more natural response from those years of experience. The breach to someone like Jake doesn’t appear like a routine thing, it’s something where he can understand all of the pieces and then wrap the security piece around it. Now it’s a matter of getting Jake’s voice heard the next time this happens, which we’re on our way to solving today.

“For learned troubleshooters,” Jonathan continued, “there isn’t this same structure or approach. Instead of doing an analysis or investigation, they’re trying to solve the problem by applying a fix that has ‘worked in the past’ before even really understanding what the problem is. Sometimes problems do get solved very quickly if their guess of what the problem is and how to resolve it is correct. But just as often, they guess the wrong thing or they haven’t really spent the time to understand what the real problem is in the first place and they end up trying to fix a problem that doesn’t exist. They don’t spend the time trying to answer my First Question: What is it? Having that answer is crucial in the troubleshooting and investigative process.”

Seeing that they had been standing around Glenn’s overly decorated office for a while now, Tim invited everyone into the nearest conference room to at least get off their feet. Outside a sunny Saturday morning had turned to rain as afternoon set in.

“Can we talk about rolling out a new server and getting the

Millennial application back online?" Tim asked Jonathan. "I want to make sure we do it right."

"Of course," Jonathan answered. "What you want is a procedure where we're not just grabbing an image and installing it.

"Right now, even if the gold image is up to date and current, it's almost inevitable that there have been new patches released by Microsoft or potentially by one of your application vendors. And the internal development team may have an update to the application. We need to go through a detailed build process which includes testing to make sure there's nothing on the system that's compromised.

"Now, let's go over composing the build book, because there are a number of steps involved," Jonathan suggested. "Hardening involves looking to make sure that all the patches are installed, uninstalling unnecessary applications, disabling or removing unnecessary services, basically ensuring that once the hardening process is complete the only things installed and running on the server need to be there. From there it's on to security policies that impose minimum password length and set up minimum enforcement policies for logging. We need to ensure there is enough space for logging, and make sure logs won't get over-written.

Tim spoke up: "You know, there are actually lots of really good examples on the Internet of build and run books. I've been in businesses where we would just go and find one that looked close to meeting our needs, customize it for our use and then make sure everybody follows them."

"That's exactly right," Jonathan responded. "Having an accessible template provides a great head start. But you still have to make sure you're working as a team on this. If you've got three guys rolling out servers, with two of them using the run book and one of them not using it, you're only as secure as whatever the third guy is doing. He's putting devices on the network that are not secured or that haven't been built using the same standards. Because what you're really ultimately trying to do with that Server Development Life Cycle is build a set of corporate standards.

"I want Glenn and Ewan to be able to say things like, 'We always build a server like this.' 'We always set up a desktop like this.' 'We always set up a network or security device like this.' It's all of those tasks.

Glenn's eyes lit up just a little. Just as he had done with Jake on security and Ewan on operations, Jonathan was engaging Glenn and providing him with a path to be a part of the solution, a part of the team. It was rewarding to Tim as the CIO to watch this unfold.

"What about when new people come on?" Ewan asked. "That always seems to be problematic. I've got the biggest team to handle of any IT manager and unfortunately we also have the highest turnover.

"That's always been the challenge of bringing in somebody new who has their own way of doing things," Jonathan responded. "Without documented processes and procedures, it's like the Wild West, each person brings what they learned at their last job into their current job. When there's a set of guidelines, it matters a lot less how they did it last time. We educate them on how Orion does things, and teach them to follow our guidelines.

"Now, the people will likely have suggestions from their past experience. 'Well, we did it this way and it actually helped a lot' so you may tune Orion's build books or run books as a result of their experience and input. But by having our own documents for them to follow it demonstrates to them that there's already a defined way of doing things here at Orion and by default we expect them to follow it. Otherwise they will immediately do things the way they did it at their last company or the way they learned it when they were in school. Meanwhile, they're breaking everything that you've spent a lot of time and money building and tuning."

"Besides us working together and having build books and run books, what other things can we be doing to avoid confusion and chaos between our groups?" Glenn asked. "Because honestly, there are a lot more problems around here that people just don't want to talk about. People have been downplaying a lot of the issues what with Tim being new here, but I can tell you that there's a real reluctance to fix any of the problems we have. Outside of this breach there are a lot of other concerns, some of them significant, and for some reason there's a real sense that fixing even the mundane things is way harder than it has to be."

Jonathan paused to think about Glenn's candid question. Glenn was opening up on some of the real issues Orion was facing, Tim thought. Of course they had tried to keep problems from him. They didn't want to be blamed or cast blame on their coworkers. Tim thought that he hadn't done a good job of getting to know the IT staff here at headquarters. He should have taken them one-by-one in for private discussions or just out to lunch to gauge their opinions of their work environment and root out some of the underlying problems. An old-timer like Glenn wasn't just going to come up to him right off the bat and tell him how frustrated everyone was. Now everything that had been festering was still there, just under the surface, and on top of that he had to deal with the Millennial meltdown.

Finally Jonathan said, "When chaos does happen, whether it's homemade or from the outside, what you don't want is to have all of that knowledge bottled up in one place. That leads companies to become dependent on these individuals who have that knowledge. Employers let them do as they please to keep them around when they should be capturing their knowledge and getting it put down on paper. Look, I know you all think you're irreplaceable but you're not. Not even Tim your boss has that luxury.

"Transferring knowledge from one person and capturing it electronically and sharing it with other people is the only way to solve this permanently," Jonathan continued. "That way the workflow of solving an IT crisis doesn't slow down by going through a single expert. It's creating multiple lanes of a stretch of highway where there used to be just one."

Tim thought of having worked with a fair number of people

who really do believe they are entitled and they put that vibe out there: "Without me, these guys would be screwed because I'm the only person who can save them. I set up all the switches and routers and firewalls and servers and I'm the only one who really knows it all." Hell, Glenn was like that! Or at least he was before Jonathan arrived on the scene and let the air out of his sails.

If getting that information out of Glenn's brain and every other Orion team member would equip the company with enough information so that even if a key person left, the business could continue on uninterrupted, it was worth the effort. As CEO, Jeff could sleep better at night knowing that all the computers and servers and databases would keep on working if any one person in IT left. Tim could sleep ever easier knowing he wouldn't be held hostage by any single IT resource. And it would help strip away any sense of exclusiveness and entitlement, and really encourage an overall sense of belonging to a team.

Tim realized that people with an attitude like this usually projected how important they were all around a company—not just to subordinates or colleagues but to bosses too. So they likely end up getting paid more than they otherwise would because they've created perceived value. The boss will justify giving them a raise rather than letting them quit and suffer potential disaster. Orion needed to eliminate the false sense of requirement associated with any single person. Getting the key information out of their heads and into a permanent tracking system was an important step in business management, and not just for IT.

Jonathan elaborated: "If it's all documented in a central document repository, if the knowledge has been shared amongst a group of people, if the team knows about it versus one person knows about it and hoards that information, then whoever you hire to fill the important roles can be cross-trained. For the security director, it doesn't mean he's going to fix the network but he will understand the logic that went in to building the network, how it's architected, and how it's being managed on an ongoing basis. We don't even have to train Jake for that because he used to work in network and systems."

Tim thought how in so many companies, that information just isn't available because it has never been documented. The network diagrams either don't exist at all or they're woefully out of date. The person holding the keys to the kingdom usually doesn't want to spend time creating the documentation because if they do they think they'll lose some or all of their power. It's the only power they have, real or perceived. They see it as real power for themselves and don't want to give it up.

"Ok," Tim interjected. "So how do you tailor an IT knowledge revamp to make it go as smoothly as possible and actually get the people with the knowledge to cooperate?" Now he didn't mind asking these questions with the prime culprits sitting around the table with him.

Jonathan's answer seemed to surprise everyone. It certainly surprised Tim.

"The reality is, it's mandated by the company and imposed across the board. Tim, it's up to you to say to everyone in IT,

'This is what we're doing and these are the reasons we're doing it.' You make it very transparent so each person understands it's not an attack on them, or an attempt to undermine their authority. You're positioning the company for future success and ensuring that IT can respond to any contingency. Any important employee could get hit by a bus tomorrow. Then what is the firm going to do?"

Tim's manager looked at one another around the conference table in a simultaneous humbling self-realization.

"You may end up where you're breaking some eggs to make an omelet," Jonathan continued. "You may end up losing an expert who has a sense of entitlement because he feels he'll no longer have his position of power. He may leave in a huff because he doesn't want to give you that information that he thinks makes him valuable. If that happens, it forces you as a company to get that information anyways.

"The amazing thing is that if that happens the fears actually start to recede, and you discover that a lot of the information you think only existed in that person can actually be recreated or captured from other sources, or wasn't nearly as critical as everyone thought it was. It's not like he was holding a button down with his finger that when removed takes the network down until somebody new comes in. Everything keeps right on working for 99.99% of companies that go through this. The doom-and-gloom scenario doesn't materialize. Human dependency is overrated and can be reduced significantly to simplify IT."

"You're not one of these people who think you can automate everything, are you?" Ewan asked. Tim was surprised by the question. He clearly was nervous about where Jonathan was taking this and wanted some clarity.

"I'm glad you asked, because the answer is an emphatic NO," Jonathan responded. "If anything, my time here should show you how much I value getting people equipped to make decisions in IT. It's not that people aren't a big part of the equation in a business, even in IT. They're the most important part of the equation, but we want to make it so that the company isn't reliant on one person or a handful of people. This helps eliminate that one person having the keys to the IT kingdom and it even helps mitigate turnover because everyone else will have a better morale under a simplified IT process. You'll end up having fewer people leaving their roles in your operations area and fewer new people coming on to replace them."

"Let me ask you this," Glenn asked Jonathan. "How is me giving up the 'keys to the kingdom' going to make me better at my job here? Right now I've got a staff of eight that works well under me. I'm rewarded by management for what we have going on here. I see how things could work better under the way you're talking about but at the end of the day why should I agree to such a radical overhaul?"

Tim looked at Glenn: he really was the ultimate "keys to the kingdom" guy here at Orion. He had been in the IT department the longest of any manager, and had the most institutional knowledge. That knowledge had effectively let him build a moat around his network and systems territory, and he got to do whatever he wanted. He had high status within the company (people upstairs in marketing and accounting seemed to know who he was), but it was obvious in this conversation that he knew IT operations were a mess at Orion. Ultimately, all the inefficiencies and points of vulnerability had to overshadow even the power he derived from his fiefdom.

Jonathan looked Glenn up and down and took a long pause before formulating his answer. He was finally faced with the sort of ultimate human resources question: why should a talented egomaniac like Glenn come on board with this power-sharing plan?

"Glenn, I could tell you that you need to get onboard with this because you'll be fired the next time something like this happens, which it will. It's obvious from your involvement prior to the breach and your post-breach response that the same strengths that make you so valuable to the company also make you a liability if you continue to operate the way you have been. But I don't want to just deal with catastrophes and hypothetical catastrophes. I want to frame this within every day, mundane IT life.

"Because here's the thing—Orion has to exist as a company going forward indefinitely, but you won't always be a part of that equation. There will come a day when you are no longer around, whether it's by your own choice or for some other reason. Like I said before: you could get hit by a bus coming to work on Monday. There have to be operational systems bigger than you that can sustain the business in your absence. That why I talked so much about build books and run books, and about processes like the Three Questions. I'm a perfectionist when it comes to meticulously setting up and maintaining processes. That should be the lifeblood of your work in network and systems and the applications you support.

"If you want to make your expertise more valuable you should want that too," Jonathan continued. "I'm not talking about in a superficial way, I'm talking about how IT actually works every day at this company. Because you can leverage your knowledge in formulating server deployment and operations life cycles. Instead of just making ad hoc decisions, you can be responsible for a whole set of processes, procedures and tasks that people will follow all the time. You'll be a part of creating a far superior system, which you'll test and validate and then help implement and train everyone to use. Doesn't that sound like a much better place to work, rather than one where everyone has to come to you for help because nothing ever works the same?"

Tim looked at Glenn and saw his head slowly nod and a smile form. This was as far as he would outwardly express satisfaction, but it seemed to signify some kind of buy-in, Tim could settle for that for now. Another keys to the kingdom convert for Jonathan. But one more important one was left.

SATURDAY, 4:12 P.M.

As Saturday dragged on, the gang huddled around a large table in Ewan's office when more staff showed up to start drafting the new build and run books. Tim excused himself after an hour or so to join a meeting with Jeff, Tina, Alex and their C-level support staff to give an update on the breach.

"Can you give us your elevator pitch on what happened to our customer data on Friday?" Jeff asked him. Tim rolled his eyes with his boss using such routine management in-speak about a cyber-security meltdown. On a certain level, the executives upstairs were still treating this like a speed bump.

"The Millennial application wasn't secure and our customer data was stolen as a result..." Tim began.

"How do you know it wasn't secure within the app?" Alex interjected. "Couldn't it have been the server or the security tool? I've heard that tool has caused other companies big problems before."

As Chief Marketing Officer, Alex had several reasons to resist the conclusion that Millennial was to blame. He had gunned hard for the app, believing that a mobile app would position Orion for the future against competing quick service restaurants. In his office he had a whiteboard list of concepts with similar apps and their start dates. Orion had little in the way of traditional marketing campaigns and the anticipation of Millennial had earned the company lots of free media coverage.

In addition, it was Alex who had brought Scott to Orion to lead the applications team and Millennial's development. Scott had worked for Alex as a vendor when Alex was at his previous company, a denim retailer. He raved about Scott's work developing a product that would let customers find the style and cut of jeans just right for them from their iPhone. Tim was always skeptical of this anecdote. As aesthetically complex as the choice of denim might be, a style guide application was a lot less complicated than an online ordering and payment product with stored personal identifiable information. It was apples to oranges. Alex was particularly taken with how clean the app looked—as a marketing guy he positioned himself as a semi-expert in graphic design—but to Tim this was a minor detail in the overall composition of the product that had far more complex challenges including security and performance.

"Because customer data was stolen and our customer data is only stored in the app," Tim responded tersely. He was out of patience with half-baked theories of the breach. Earlier that afternoon in the cafeteria someone from communications suggested to him that it might have been done by ISIS.

"The banking system holds our customers' conventional credit card swipe data," Tim continued. "We talked to them first thing yesterday and ruled that out. None of our employees' personal information was affected, so we know it wasn't an intrusion with our internal servers here at headquarters. It has to be the application, there's no other source of customer information and credit card data that matches the data that was leaked."

Alex had a scowl on his face. Tina was already upset that Terry, his pricey talking head "crisis consultant," had been sidelined thanks to Tim's interference. Jeff was still edgy about Tim's own consultant. Despite all they'd accomplished downstairs that weekend, no one around the table was cheered up at all.

"So how's this friend of yours doing?" Jeff asked Tim. "What have you guys been burrowing through down there?"

Tim relished the chance to update them on Jonathan's work over the last 36 hours. He told them about empowering Jake for the first time to do security protocol, about the scene in Ewan's operations unit with the hapless managed security provider's people, the way Jake and Ewan would now work together on important security operations like testing and patching, and how Glenn had finally assented to giving up immediate control of his turf in order to make things work smoothly with server deployment life cycle.

"So then have you blown up the development shop yet?" Jeff asked. He was starting to enjoy this while Alex let out a sigh and grew more visibly displeased.

"That's next," Tim answered.

"Well if you think development is the source of the problem why didn't you go there first?" Alex demanded.

Tim was ready for this question. "To be honest," he responded—looking straight at Alex—"Scott is the most isolated and autonomous of anyone under my review, and his team is at the center of the meltdown. Jonathan wanted to get everyone else on board before we talked to Scott, so we can have a productive discussion and explain to him how development can work with the rest of the IT team. There's no guarantee he'll buy in like the rest of them have, but this way is our best shot. We shut down the application before store openings yesterday so right now this isn't an issue of time, we're focusing on making sure this can't happen again."

"Well, it is an issue of timing if we want to start monetizing this!" a voice piped up from the speakerphone in the middle of the table. It was the company's COO Doug Martin. Tim hated it when there were people unannounced on the speakerphone in meetings.

"Doug, I know this product was developed to hook in customers and have a large return on investment," Tim replied in as restrained manner as he could muster. "But the company's approach to development is so misaligned that unless I focus on fixing it now with the consultant here we won't get Millennial back online or have any new products for the foreseeable future. So all our work this weekend so far has been a build-up to the hardest and most complex task of all, which is getting development working right with the rest of IT. That's why I've been so methodical about it."

Doug didn't say anything, which was his way of conceding the point. "Roger that," said Jeff. "Good luck dealing with this Scott rascal, Tim." His Texas drawl materialized for the first time Tim had known him. "You and your guy have gotten the other IT outlaws on board. What's the trick up your sleeve for dealing with this one?"

"Something called DevOps," Tim replied confidently. It was clear from their blank faces no one in the room had heard of the term.

Back downstairs, Jonathan and the gang had already migrated over to the development corridor where Scott and his team of six programmers worked. In between three large desks they shared for their workstations was a large conference table with empty pizza boxes, candy wrappers, and soda bottles strewn around. All the junk covered the speakerphone in the middle. It was messier than Ewan's operations section, which was saying something. Tim thought back to the all-hands IT meeting he held when he first arrived at Orion and none of the developers had come to it. Even Glenn had bothered to show up to that one. These guys projected the least amount of respect for authority or teamwork on the floor.

Scott looked like the stereotypical computer hacker from nineties film or television; wiry figure, unbuttoned oxford shirt over a t-shirt, bad haircut and glasses to complete the look. Tim had done some digging and learned he'd done good work building custom software for clients in the retail space. But he'd never been a development lead before and had never had to integrate his products with operations or security the way that Millennial demanded. The six people he hired at Orion were all minions of his from prior outside projects. One was even imported from Belarus after Scott had used him so much via long distance. They seemed alert and receptive, especially considering it was a weekend.

Tim had expected to hear yelling, or at least audible tension, when he entered the space like he had before when he left Jonathan and one of his department leads to go at it. But instead he found Jonathan talking to Scott in a measured tone. It actually sounded a bit like people talking in the library.

"Scott, you're the most important person in the building right now. If we're going to fix the mess from yesterday and IT here in general, you've got to be at the center of it. Tell me why you think that is. Why are you as the applications developer likely best positioned to address it?"

"Ah..." Scott stammered, not sure if this label was a good thing or a bad thing yet. "Well, obviously the breach has to do with the product we made, so..."

"Hold on, I'm not trying to pin this all on you. I'm singling you out because as the head of application development you're someone who spends his time building new software programs. You're in possession of the most relevant knowledge of what the breach is targeting if it's in the applications world—which we know it is. You've got more inside your head about it than anybody here. You know how the customers' credit cards are ingested, how they process it, and where it's stored."

"Right."

"Scott, even though this whole mess has the potential to make national news and sink the company, I've got a different theory for why development failed the company.

"You're getting a little mercy from me because I see this at just about every organization I get called into," Jonathan continued. "Granted, only the companies facing real challenges decide to invest the money to hire me, but these are all established companies that are making money and getting good press just like yours; it's the IT management they can't get straight and it has the potential to sabotage them just like it has here.

"What happens in a lot of organizations is the network and systems people don't want the applications team touching the production systems. They say, 'We're responsible for the performance. We're responsible for the availability of all the things that are there so we don't want you screwing with our systems. You give us the code. We'll put it online. We'll take care of rolling the application out. We do all that.' They want the developers to just throw the application over the fence to them so they can take it from there. It's the silo system."

"Yeah, we definitely have the silo system here," Scott interjected. This was a bit rich, Tim thought, considering it was Scott's team that isolated themselves from everyone during the Millennial development process and didn't show up at his all-hands IT meeting. He couldn't let that initial blow off go.

"And you developers typically don't do them any favors because you don't want to get involved in operations! That's a world you're not part of and don't understand. You want to focus on satisfying the requirements that the company set for this application. You're also disconnected from network and systems. It's a two-way street," Jonathan returned.

Thank you for setting him straight, Tim thought.

Jonathan got up from his swivel chair and approached the nearest white board.

"Alright, let's diagram the people in place around an application. There is the operations guy who's got to run the network. Then there are the developers whose application has got to work on the network. There's the systems guy who's responsible for making sure the application works properly on the network. Then there's the security guy who's trying to secure the application, the servers and the network. These groups should be working together, not communicating to one another at crude handoffs.

"What happens instead in companies is there's a lot of dictating back and forth. The application developers will dictate to the operations or systems people a list of things they need, like a certain server and storage size. Those on the receiving end will dictate back to the developers the parameters they need for the program to get it up and running. Those developers just focus on coding what they're supposed to build. From what Tim told me, Scott, you and your team just hunkered down in your bunker over here and didn't engage with the outside IT world at Orion when you were building this app."

Scott looked sideways at Tim, who stared stoically back. I'm not letting you off the hook on this one, Tim thought.

"Fine, guilty as charged," Scott replied while raising his right hand. "But what's your alternative for how it's supposed to go? My team—we get our orders to code a program, we try and do what we're asked because we're the only ones here who can do it. It's honestly a lot of incoming we're taking from the other departments here—do this, now do that!—especially from Glenn. So I don't see how we're supposed to operate any differently to survive under these tough conditions. It's what I've always done working in development."

"Well I appreciate your candor, Scott," Jonathan responded. "And I'm glad you prompted me for a holistic answer because that's why I came here, not to just diagnose the problem but to give you a way to fix it. So let's talk about DevOps."

Finally, Tim thought. They were getting to his big deliverable for Jeff: systematically revamping IT at Orion.

"I was at an IT conference right after the market crashed in 2008," Jonathan began. "Everyone in technology was bemoaning the lack of capital available. No one wanted to invest in anything. They couldn't get venture capital firms to let them in the door to raise money. It was depressing, and you could have talked yourself into the idea that tech was basically over. But a funny thing happened there and during that time when the money froze up. Those of us in development and operations got together and brainstormed about how to work more efficiently and effectively, how to use what we had at our disposal to do our best work. The recession really gave us a chance to hit the reset button and redesign how IT could function best. Since no new money was coming in to fund projects, we had the time to pause and think about the big picture."

Now Tim was really glued to Jonathan—he hadn't heard this backstory before.

"It kind of started with the mission to do more with less," Jonathan continued. "We realized that we couldn't just do the waterfall method anymore."

The waterfall method is a structured approach to development that mandates blueprinting the program out and then building it methodically. Tim considered it a relic of the past because it was slow and put off testing until the end. Its sequential nature, with the division of labor like an assembly line, also encouraging the silo formation of IT teams that Orion was plagued by. *Making perfect the enemy of the good* was the cliché Tim and many others in his position applied to it.

"We had to go lean and cut corners," Jonathan said. "No longer could we afford this drawn-out approach to development that pivoted from team to team. There were no teams left at some companies! We had to get everyone involved in building a product rather than just as part of a step along the way. So we embraced the agile method."

Agile development had emerged over the years as the counter to waterfall: an incremental and informal approach to building applications that asked people to work together and go fast. All the high-flyers in tech used it, but not the companies Tim had worked for where IT was supplemental rather than central to the business model.

"So we knew if we we're going to be using agile we had to have a larger philosophy for IT that reflected how we did development," Jonathan went on. "How was everything going to fit together if we were going to embrace the fast pace and sometimes even mad environment of agile?

"The idea of DevOps really helps with this. For the developer, it means, philosophically and practically, working with the operations guys. *Cross-functioning*. Just like the workout program CrossFit involves exercises to work both the heart and the muscles, cross-functioning means development and operations working together simultaneously. They're working together using an automated process to roll the application out in a consistent, reliable, repeatable fashion. When it's tested, they test it together along the way rather than putting off testing to its own phase at the end. Both sides are plugged in to what is going on with the development and operation of the application.

"DevOps provides the opportunity to automate the IT division of labor. It flows from the application team into the operations team and they work together to roll it out. *Automation* rather than *separation* is the key. There's no point in time where responsibility over an application ever ends because each IT team is engaged in it throughout to fix whatever falls in their zone of responsibility.

"Tim—that means you make development involved in deployment. In turn, development principles are applied to deployment so that an application's rollout is systematized and goes much smoother. Ewan isn't winging it anymore; he's working with a product that has rules for the road in operating. The torch is passed to operations seamlessly without the back-and-forth or arbitrary handoffs that characterize the traditional divisions between development and operations."

"How do we start to formalize this?" Scott asked. "I can't just start working with Ewan like everything's cool and we have a rapport all of a sudden."

"Now you're thinking in the right direction," Jonathan replied. "For one thing, let's start with both of your teams sitting closer to each other, literally. I want all your developers to move alongside Ewan's space, because he has room to accommodate you over there and you don't have room to accommodate his gang. Then I want you to do a dry run of a software application's development where you both cover step-by-step the things that need to happen and where operations needs to be involved in practices testing and validating. Some of it you'll need to compromise with each other on—and I think that will help you to start to build a rapport. You and Ewan should both take detailed notes on everything you agree to, so you'll have this as a roadmap for how to work together."

"Okay, I can live with that," Scott said.

Only Jonathan's detailed instructions for sharing responsibility and planning could get Scott to agree to this experiment so readily, Tim thought.

"Let's get specific on security," Jonathan continued. "The best way to start thinking about introducing DevOps is with the Software Development Life Cycle. As a developer this is your build book. The SDLC tells the applications team when they start to design something that security is involved from the very beginning and is built into the product's architecture. When the code reaches a certain level of sophistication, it tells you to run it through static code analysis to look for vulnerabilities in the code. That's done once a week, once a month, once per quarter—whatever pace corresponds with your development of the code. The idea is to snuff out any security vulnerabilities long before the product launches. That's what Millennial really needed!

"Look, Scott, I know you are not in the information security business like Jake. What gets you out of bed in the morning is building killer products and perfecting the graphical user interface; all that hoopla. One of the challenges for getting developers to think about security risks is that they aren't used to appreciating the ramifications of them because it's not part of their core business of making things. Companies often get a list of bugs in a new product—there could be 300 bugs—and they lay it on the applications team's to-do list to fix. Meanwhile, if the product has already launched those bugs have given way to security vulnerabilities. It's akin to seeing that the lock on the back door has been broken, and making a reminder to yourself to call the lock guy. By treating it as a mundane task, management and the developers shrug off security."

Mundane—that's the way the people up in the C-level certainly viewed IT security until yesterday, Tim thought.

"Teaching secure coding to developers—which can be done by a security consultant—is another way to get them to appreciate what bugs can mean and what happens if somebody exploits them," Jonathan went on. "This learning process opens their eyes in so many ways because they don't really understand the significance or the impact of what that vulnerability is. Because to developers, writing insecure code is like a spelling mistake or dialing the wrong phone number. Another bug that you need to fix. I'm channeling a sense of urgency into it.

"With secure coding principles your programmers will start to understand, 'Wait a second. You mean they can see all the data in the database? They can log in as one person but use someone else's credentials to access information?' That's when their eyes really open up, when you see a fellow developer doing it and it's even more impactful when it's happening on their own application."

Tim wanted to bring up something he thought essential for Jonathan to debunk: recycling bad code. In his experience he had seen developers fall into the bad habit of taking open source code off the Internet and deploying it in their applications without testing it for faults.

"How does code reuse figure into this?" Tim posed to Jonathan.

"Code reuse is a big problem for secure coding," he replied. "Developers are just as lazy as any other types of people at times. They'll go on the Internet and look at what has been built before to serve their function. They'll modify the code snippet as needed and apply it to their application, having just saved themselves hours of time recreating code for that simple function.

"What they don't realize is the guy who wrote that snippet of code threw it together four or five years ago and didn't realize that he left some type of a vulnerability in there. Now that vulnerability is in 72 different lines in the application because the developer used it repeatedly where it was needed. We see that over and over and over again in applications. Normally when you find insecure code you find it riddled throughout the application. It's not usually just in one spot.

"It compounds the problem as well because a hacker can identify replicated or similar points of weakness for entry. He finds, for example, the 'forgot password' page and is able to pull information from it. Next he's going to look for that particular weakness every other time, every other place in your application he can find. He may compromise you in four or five, or 10 or 20 different places because you've got that same vulnerability all over the place and the forgot password page was just the first place he found it. Code reuse can be deadly when it comes to distributing vulnerabilities throughout an application."

"Hold on, Jonathan," Scott interjected. "I don't think we could even do our jobs here without grabbing code from somewhere. It saves us from reinventing the wheel every time."

"I agree with you!" Jonathan retorted. "Code reuse is also a massive shortcut that if used properly is wonderful.

"Take SQL. Structured Query Language is the most common programming language used with databases. In the SQL world we talk about things called stored procedures. It's one of the ways that they protect SQL. SQL is a bunch of commands—queries that talk to data and make it to do a bunch of things. In SQL itself it is usually not that difficult to modify those commands and get it to do things that you don't want it to do.

"A stored procedure on the other hand, when written properly, only allows you to do exactly what that stored procedure is supposed to do and then you pass parameters for that stored procedure. If you have to get a hundred different things from the database, you could either write a hundred different discreet SQL commands and lay them all out and have a hundred chances to screw the code up, or write one stored procedure really, really well and use that procedure and pass parameters to accomplish those same 100 things that you want to do in the database.

"So the stored procedure—the idea of doing it once and reusing it over and over—is pervasive throughout all software development. That's the model for reusing code, Scott. But if you have an insecure piece of code and you're using it over and over again, it just exacerbates the problem."

"Let's get even more basic than that with the SDLC," Jonathan continued. "Because there are perfunctory tasks in keeping applications secure that developers overlook. For instance, when they set up an input validation, like a password, there could be a vulnerability point in every field. A hacker could use a script to break through the field. That's why the SDLC is used to stipulate a set of rules for each field. Whether each password is always a combination of the 26 alphabet letters and 10 digits, or only phone number structures are allowed in the phone field, it minimizes the ability of intruders to mess around with that input.

"The SDLC should be built with a set of parameters for things like fields as well as a glossary of terms. First of all, we don't want Scott's people wasting time having to look for those things. But more importantly is construct: we want every developer to know that each element of the application is constructed a certain way where he can see how each term to go with it is defined. It's a set of rules to live by that are defined at the beginning of the application building process. Before a single line of code is ever written, you've laid down as many of those rules as you possibly can so that the developers understand what to do and what not to do when they're coding."

Tim loved this preparation in developing applications that Jonathan emphasized. Too many programmers just wanted to start building their assignments, grabbing code from wherever they could. The DevOps paradigm focusing on the SDLC was meant to head off all the mistakes that could happen at the beginning. In a way, it wasn't just derived from the agile method, but the waterfall method as well because it had the methodical nature to it that comes with the SDLC.

"Jonathan, how should Scott's team and Jake interact," Tim asked. Tim wanted Scott to be able to get a picture of how close development and security would actually work together on the next application.

"Oh, make no mistake," Jonathan replied. "You still need the information security team at the table during development, with their influence in the process. The SDLC is a document, and human guidance is needed to ensure compliance with it. The security guys are the ones who will remind the developers, 'Are we remembering that the password has to change every three months?' Or, 'How many different requirements are going into the password field?'"

> This kind of planning and teamwork is a simple approach to bridge the divide between developers who are inclined toward product openness and security experts who value encryption. The more the two sides communicate, the more these biases will soften up and they'll both be able to approach the development of an application with the holistic goal of having it functional **and** secure.

"Let's talk sessions," Jonathan said, pivoting in his chair to emphasize the change of subject. Sessions are the connections that take place between services and ports on servers and users or other services.

"One breach in the IT world we security consultants see on a regular basis has to do with sessions. When a user fires up their web browser, it creates one or more sessions to the web server that it's talking to. When an application talks to a database to gather information it creates a session to do so. When you connect to an application, you're assigned a session ID. Now obviously the user wouldn't know that because they're using a web browser and not seeing it but in the background there's a session ID. That ID is used to allow the application to differentiate between each user upon their connection. You follow me, Scott?"

Scott nodded his head yes.

"One common intrusion is session persistence—that's where you've decided you're done with the application, but the application doesn't know that. We've all had the experience where we've gone onto another webpage, but the application has kept us logged in because it thinks we just accidentally hit the back button or something like that. So if a hacker can figure out your session ID number by following your trail, then they may be able to assume your identity for that application. They're just logging in after you've logged out, or thought you did.

"We also see something called session fixation and crossover," Jonathan continued. "Once the hacker gets your session ID, they connect to the application and then connect and close it repeatedly. They'll do that five or ten times and look to see what other session IDs they get. It's looking for a pattern. If you're number one and they connect five times in a row to get IDs two, three, four, five, seven, the odds are pretty good you logged in. Maybe you were ID six but now they know exactly what the sequence is of people logging in so it's inevitable there's going to be an eighth login. Knowing this total lets them prey on other users and their session IDs in the application.

"Finally, there's another problem called session reuse. The same logic applies. The hacker might connect to your application ten times, 100 times, 1,000 times, even 10,000 times, and each time is getting a unique session out of it. They're looking to see if the application is reusing any of those session IDs. An application developer may only use a pool of 10,000 sessions, and repeatedly calling up new sessions lets the hacker figure out how many exactly so he can sequence and locate them."

"So what's your solution for dealing with sessions?" Scott asked.

"Your developers should be putting in randomized sessions so the hackers don't have any way of dissecting patterns through reuse," Jonathan replied. "That way as the hackers log in and out and accumulate session IDs to test there is no pattern to the IDs that could enable them to figure it out."

It was great to see someone who Tim thought of as unwilling to learn taking this all in, absorbing lessons to apply to his work. Just as important, it was gratifying to see that this cross-functional learning could take place. For Jake, these security issues were standard, but not for a developer like Scott. If the developers could learn how to *think* like Jake when programming applications, Orion's IT department would multiply in terms of effectiveness. There wouldn't be the walls holding the silos for each unit; instead the teams would work side-by-side and do many of the same things: Scott would be accountable for ensuring there was sufficient security in the apps, Ewan would be responsible for running operations with the speed and flexibility of a development shop, Jake would be responsible for making the security tools function, and Glenn would make sure the network architecture worked for all of this to go smoothly. The whole department would work as a high-tech factory in churning out complex products.

Engaged with Jonathan's talking points, Scott asked him to keep going and explain harder-to-detect security threats. "What should keep us up at night?" he asked.

"Actually, when the application is updated" Jonathan responded. "There are many commercial and open source tools for version control—the system that controls and keeps track of changes to an application over time. But many companies don't have version control tools. The developers end up with different versions of their code amongst them, and none of it is centralized. This creates its own keys-to-the-kingdom effect where each developer with essential or updated code has control over it, rather than the updated code all being in one place. You want all that code in one place.

"Version control enables a central repository of changes—and therefore lets you label an application version 1.0 then 1.1 and onward. The phrasing used is 'checking in' and 'checking out' code. So if a developer is working on a particular module today, you know that he logs into the version control system and he checks out the latest version. Other people working on the code know that he's also now working on it. It doesn't mean they all can't work on it simultaneously but the system prevents them from overwriting each other. It keeps things in a sequence and tracks the changes."

"So it's kind of like Google Docs?" Scott asked.

"Exactly. Documentation is just as important as version control for building an application. During a security breach of an application, if nothing has been documented, how do you know where to start? There could be 250,000 lines of code. That's why documentation both outside the application and inside the application is so important."

"How do you do it as consultants?" Scott asked. "If you're working for different clients all the time how do you keep those tasks organized? Because we face the same kind of challenge in-house here at Orion with different projects thrown at us."

"We have a very large repository of documentation in our consulting world," Jonathan answered. "We document *everything*. We also make diagrams and build prototypes and have what we call functional specifications. Those are made with the people on the business side of the application and describe in almost excruciating detail how each thing is supposed to work. Then the developers build technical documentation, which describes how they're going to code those particular things. Ideally that leaves you with high-level design comments. There's a well-designed and laid out prototype of some type. There's functional specifications and there's technical specifications. Only once all of that is done does anybody start writing code."

"Yeah, up 'til now we'd done it a little more casual than that," Scott said to chuckles around the room. Even Tim could laugh at his honesty.

"Let's talk methods of development," Jonathan continued. "As you know, there are two general approaches to writing code: waterfall and agile. The traditional one is the waterfall methodology. That's a blueprint for building an application like a waterfall—starting at the top and flowing down—built in sync from beginning to end. The development team builds all of what the business people have described what they need built to a T. So if it's a two-year project, they've laid out everything they're going to do for the next two years to get to completion.

"Agile, on the other hand, is focused on effectiveness rather than symmetry. It says, 'We want to get started, let's go; let's be nimble and get this product to market.' You may start with 100 things that the application needs to do, but shift to thinking about the Minimum Viable Product that needs 10 basic functions to be working. So those first 10 functions get built, the application can be deployed and users can start using it. And then development continues on to tackle the 90 remaining functions. MVP is typically defined in software development as what an application needs to be at a basic minimum in order for it to be sold or provided to the end users. The rest of the functions are released along the way as updates.

"The process in agile development of prioritizing and concentrating on building chosen functions to maximize effectiveness is called a sprint. There may be four sprints over two months, with breaks in between to decide what to build next. Each day there is a 'scrum meeting' to answer these three questions: 'What did we do yesterday? What are we going to do today? Is there anything preventing us from getting the job done?'

"Do you have scrum meetings with your guys here Scott?"

"Semi-regularly," Scott answered. "Sometimes we just get so bogged down in our own coding assignments we let them go for a while."

"Well scrum meetings are just as important as coding itself, actually more important because they are a prerequisite to good coding," Jonathan said. "Each developer needs to answer the scrum meeting questions before going off to do their work for the day. The next morning you rinse and repeat. So in the agile methodology you use the documentation process to build out the stories that describe what the features and functions are and the sprint steps are used to answer those stories.

The complication with the agile method is the remaining functions that didn't get planned out yet. The developer may not even be aware of how many functions are left to build in the application, if they haven't been documented yet. Or they just aren't really clear. So they're in the middle of building those core first 10 functions and then hear about the next 10 coming down the line. Sometimes they'll respond, "Well if I had known about that, I would have built these functions totally differently!" So in some cases there is a lot of code that gets built and used for a period of time and then thrown away. There may also be a need to go back and insert rules for security that get added along the way, so that can result in code getting tossed as well. In the waterfall approach you rarely see that happen because you know about all the features in advance in all their detail, including security requirements.

Whereas most applications used to be built the waterfall way, agile has surpassed it in popularity. Today developers are embracing a hybrid approach of waterfall and agile. They define most of the project but build it using sprints. Everybody has a basic understanding of what the whole project is going to do and they understand what the basic functions are going to be, even though they haven't got all the documented specifications. They have enough of a roadmap to build functions that will integrate with the rest of them down the line, resulting is less requirements to go back and rebuild code. The hybrid practice combines the methodical approach of waterfall with the effectiveness of agile.

In the development world, unlike brain surgery, there's not one right way to do something. That's why there are so many differences of opinion in the approach to building applications. But the most basic principle for making differences of opinion less of an issue is version control.

"There's a reason for all this diligence," Jonathan continued. "The way that I coded it may be totally different from the way you would have coded it, although we would both end up with the same end result. As developers we have a tendency to disparage other developers' code. 'This is garbage. I could have done this in 10 lines of code and they used 200.' But if there's no documentation you usually don't know the context. They don't know why that developer built it that way without those comments there to help people understand what it is they're looking at and how it ties everything together. Lack of documentation can be a major problem with developers leaving or changing roles on the development team.

"Code notation is an important piece of the version control because it supports the tracking of all the changes and features in each version. Version control really helps to understand, obviously, what version you're working with and what each version is doing. The documentation helps to understand from a bigger picture what it is that we're actually building and then the notation inside the code itself helps to understand what each piece of code that you're working on does so you don't have to waste time trying to figure that out. It's the proper commenting inside the software itself so you know what each piece of code does, who wrote it and when it was first created. Just those one line comments all the way through make it so much easier for people to troubleshoot the code and get on with life if somebody leaves. Scott, how often does a developer of yours leave for another position?"

"Seems about once every three months or so," Scott responded.

"Wow, high rate of attrition for such a small staff! Well if somebody leaves and hands you their code, they know it inside out, backwards, and sideways. But you don't without the documentation and notation. So it will take you a long time to really try to unravel what they gave you on the way out.

"Let me tell you a story of how I once lost around a million dollars on bad code."

Everyone's eyes lit up, as if the idea of Jonathan making such a costly mistake was unthinkable.

"My company did a massive development endeavor of the

last version of our software that we primarily outsourced to a vendor. We had significant challenges, cost overruns, all kinds of things happened. The vendor struggled. Eventually we brought a new guy in with the idea of him managing the outsourced team and helping to get the project back on track. Within the first month, he came to me and said, 'I basically can't work with the code.' Again, developers tend to be dismissive of other people's code but I also knew there were real challenges with what they had done. He did not trust the code at all. He didn't believe that he was going to be able to take that code and do something with it.

"We were going to hire our own developers and take that code back and somehow fix it. He said, 'If you tell me I have to work with this code, I'll take it but I don't trust it because I don't understand it. A lot of stuff that I see just doesn't make sense. I can't ultimately be accountable for this software because you're asking me to build on top of stuff that somebody else spent almost two years building. And now you want me to take it and fix it and turn it into something else. We're far better off throwing it away and starting from scratch.'

"So, wow, right?" Jonathan continued. "This guy felt he was going to spend far more time having to rebuild or fix things they had built than us simply building it ourselves. It cost my firm just over a million dollars to junk that code. Ultimately we had to write it all off. Code write-off happens all the time in development at far larger stakes than what I went through, especially when you see software companies buying each other. From the outside we assume during these acquisitions that they bought the target company and have taken their code and rolled it on. But in many cases they never use a line of the code from the product they got in the deal. They took the functionality, the ideas, and everything else and they either rebuilt it or they modified their application to do it.

"Let me ask you, Scott, when you buy software here at Orion do you get it from the large vendors or the small ones?"

"Ah, when we do that it's always the large software vendors," Scott responded.

"And why is that? What is it about the large ones that make them preferable to the small ones?"

"Honestly, it's not the products per se. It's that people not in IT know the brand names and therefore approve of them."

"Exactly!" Jonathan grew excited. "These firms are essentially marketing companies. They are in the business of selling and billing. CIOs feed into their strategy because they admire the seal of approval that the big firms come with. In the technology world there's the saying that nobody ever got fired for buying IBM or nobody ever got fired for buying Cisco. In the security world it used to be that nobody ever got fired for buying Checkpoint. That was the firewall of choice at one point in time.

"But let me tell you something," he continued, looking at both Scott and Tim. "That single-vendor mentality has changed because people are actually being fired now for betting on the wrong horse. The bias is still there to do business with the big firms because of the status they confer, but now there's more accountability for what IT managers choose to buy. There's more quality control and scrutiny of big software projects going on, especially with high-profile disasters like the U.S. government's Healthcare.gov platform and the Target breach. Or Millennial now." He suppressed a smile.

"Yeah," Scott interjected, "but when a division like mine is tasked with taking a corporate vision and turning it into a usable software application, that's where a lot of the problems come in. It's either over-architected—which is what I know you were talking about with Healthcare.gov—or underwhelming.

"We developers get hit with 11th hour changes all the time. For instance, when we first started selling gift cards online the marketing department wanted a webpage built so that so-called loyalty members could sign into an authenticated landing page and be able to get better deals on gift cards than non-loyalty members. We talked at length about the sign up process. We talked at length about the payment process for buying the gift cards. But they didn't tell us until *after* the application was delivered that they wanted PayPal capability in the application. So my team had to go back and install PayPal and absorb the time overrun since it wasn't in the wireframes we set up in advance. Sometimes marketing thinks features are assumed or don't need to be mentioned, so they don't bring them up until it's too late."

Tim hadn't heard this story before, but it certainly didn't surprise him. He had worked with a lot of development shops in the past—the types of places where Scott once worked—to build workflow applications for his old firm. These were relatively small products, but skating by even seemingly little things like visibility settings for comments or export file functions tripped them up. The cost overruns annoyed the hell out of Tim's bosses. After a while it seemed like the way of life in software development.

Realizing he had the same experience and attitude as Scott on this, just from the other side of things, he pressed his case to Jonathan.

"Jonathan, how do we break free of this dynamic where it's like we are hostage to the business people asking for the software?" Tim asked. "We're at their whim on every additional function they demand along the way?"

"That's why it's in the developers' interest to have as much specificity from the client upfront, accomplished through automation and then fully documented and agreed to," Jonathan answered. "Like I mentioned earlier, there are the technical specs and the functional specs. When a client works with a developer to build out a set of functional specs, it's really an opportunity for the client to say, 'Here's what I want you to build.' They don't need to see the technical specs because they are intended to be used by the developer to understand how they're going to build it. So if they didn't have PayPal in that set of functional specs, then the developers are going to build the application without it, and if they really want or need it, the developers have an opportunity to push back.

"In software development, there are typically three factors that come into play: time, features, and budget. When we first start to design an application, we figure out what it needs to do: the features. Then we figure out how much time it's going to take us to build each feature. And we typically use that information to prepare a budget. Assuming everyone is in agreement with the estimates for all three items, the project gets started. But what happens when something changes. Suddenly the time estimate to complete a feature doubles or triples. This means that it will take more time to finish the application, so the ship date may slip, and it means that it will cost more money to complete the application, so the budget needs to increase. These three factors are a constant struggle to keep in check with any software development project, as in almost all cases, one, two, or even all three of them have to change in order to get the development project complete.

"This also contributes to how security can get left out in development. Just like PayPal wasn't there for your gift card page, if the client doesn't ask for something as simple as authentication then those user name and password fields aren't going to be there. It's a step that has to happen in both the functional specifications that the developers get from the client and the Software Development Life Cycle that they build to run the application."

"How do you hardwire security in the functional specs?" Tim asked. "Because you're saying if it's not in those it's not getting into the application."

"Oh, that may be the biggest challenge in this whole ballgame," Jonathan responded. "Because the performance metrics the business-facing people demand during the application development can pose major threats to security. Let's face it: product enhancement or security is one of the easiest trade-offs that you can make. It's part of a mindset that says, 'We'll put that in later.' A firm says it wants two factor authentication in there from day one, but when they see that it takes an extra six months to build they decide to go live without it and put it in later. Of course, the functionality either never comes or maybe it comes only when it's too late. The business people only think about going to market so they can generate the return on their investment in the software. There can also be so many other timing concerns on their plate in addition to revenue for that software launch: media, investor relations, the board of directors. Security to them is in that nebulous zone between an essential function and a luxury. So they skimp on emphasizing to developers like Scott what the security features should be.

"Those of us in high-level information security consulting see it all the time. We get the call at the 11th hour. They're going live tomorrow and need somebody to test their application. They've had t-shirts printed up. The press release was sent out. They thought their security guys were testing the application but they never did. Now they want us to do a quick down-and-dirty penetration test to let them know if there are any problems. Of course there are problems. But 99 out of 100 times, they go live anyways."

Tim's anger resurfaced as his thoughts drifted upstairs to Alex and the marketing department. He tried to refocus back into the meeting.

"Then they'll scramble to try to fix any of them they think they can or they put in a compensating control," Jonathan continued. "Maybe they put a web application firewall in front. They'll do something that doesn't involve changing the application, but at the end of day they still end up going live with an insecure application and they know the application is insecure and yet they're allowing customers to sign up. They're letting customers put confidential information in and process orders through it because at the end of the day they justify that they've got to make money.

"As the security director, Jake should be at the very first meeting to design it. Because before the marketing people and whoever else even start to talk about the colours and the look and the appearance of the application, the developers need to have an architecture discussion with him involved. Then they meet with the people upstairs to thoroughly go over the functional specs and see if Jake approves. When you put security into the foundation of the application right off the bat, then you know that when you build on top of it the security is embedded right in it. That's so much better than bolting security fixes on top after it's complete."

"What is wrong with 'bolting on' per se?" Scott asked. "I've seen some pretty good security features added after creating programs and it seems like the right way to finish off a product before it ships. Plus, we can move faster in the beginning if we're not bogged down in security discussions outside of development."

Scott obviously figured it was more convenient for him to

develop the application and then hand if off to Jake to secure. This was probably more efficient than the way Jonathan was proposing, but was it effective? Tim wondered.

"Hold on, Scott"—Jonathan pushed back—"When you bolt something on there are two major risks: A) it can be knocked right off or B) it can be worked around. Security bolt-on's are not that difficult to find because they're not embedded. They're not part of the foundation so they're more noticeable. They are superficial add-ons that make a hacker smile when he sees them, because he's confident that he can slip through them or work around them.

"And look—the security team doesn't have to be there at every meeting. They're obviously not sitting and coding every day. But they should be there at the very beginning when the planning happens. Jake and his staff are there to review and finalize the security-related architecture, plans and documents that your developers will use after that."

"Okay, so Jake doesn't have to be at every planning meeting?" Scott was still slightly worried about this, probably a good thing, Tim thought.

"If you're using agile development, then someone from the security team is at some of the scrum meetings. He's at the kick-off of each sprint—where the individual functions are built—so he understands what's being built and can identify where security may need to play a role. Then he's at the sprint wrap-up to assess how the security components got done. He's responsible for ensuring the security features that were agreed upon in the plans exist and are functional in the completed code. That way you don't bypass something critical like SSL when you're getting ready for the next sprint. Scott, having Jake around to think through these things and remind you to program them in as you go along and build the app's core functions will actually make your life *easier* rather than harder."

Scott wasn't protesting this one, and finally appeared content with Jonathan's blueprint for a somewhat radical overhaul of development at Orion. Tim was initially worried about Scott and Jake butting heads on this new method for integrating security with development but now he realized that each would be happier with this process, even if it meant the two of them spending more time together.

It was a balanced approach—development would have to slow down a bit but their products would end up more credible. Security would have actual influence on the software—unlike with Millennial. The business people upstairs would have to really map out the applications they wanted instead of assuming features would be included or getting away with being vague or indecisive on the wireframes. Everyone would do a little extra work in this method but they would be oriented away from the screw-ups, delays, overruns, and breaches that mar in-house software development. It was a method that combined effectiveness with security. After associating the combination of the two words *Orion* and *security* with embarrassment and guilt, Tim finally had a reason to use them with the confidence that comes from having a plan.

SATURDAY, 7:18 P.M.

The session in Scott's development den was exhausting. Afterward even the seemingly indefatigable Jonathan looked worn out. Joined by Scott, Ewan, Glenn and Jake, they repaired to the company canteen to find a buffet of rib eye steaks, mashed potatoes, and macaroni and cheese. Seemingly out of nowhere, Jeff popped in and announced that he'd heard how intense they were working and wanted to give them something better than pizza for their dinner. Tim was grateful for the nourishment but wondered where Jeff had heard about anything going on with them since they'd been cloistered all afternoon downstairs. Maybe this was the upside of having interlopers in IT communicating with the C-suite.

The crew ate voraciously, mostly in silence, heartened by the solid meal. As they finished, Jeff got up to excuse himself when Jonathan grabbed him by the arm and stopped him.

"I'd like to request you stay for our last meeting tonight. It's really important and we need the CEO to be involved in this one."

Jeff looked stunned, having figured he'd done his nice gesture for the evening. He looked at Tim for approval and Tim gave him a nod. "Well, I hadn't planned on it and don't want to get in the way of an honest discussion among you all, but if you want me here okay, I'm all yours."

"Don't worry about interfering with an honest discussion, Jeff! We want you to be a part of it."

Jeff smiled and looked puzzled. Aside from the occasional comedian brought into corporate retreats organized by the HR staff, he was unused to eccentric outsiders taking control of company meetings. During a day of managers' undressing at the hands of Jonathan, even the CEO wasn't spared.

After everyone finished the meal they all repaired downstairs to the main IT conference room. Jonathan had gone ahead to write some notes on the white board, which contained a matrix below "DevOps" in large letters. Jeff walked in and looked like he was trying to read a foreign language.

"Whatever it is, this looks expensive," Jeff half-joked.

"Relax, Jeff," Jonathan answered. "DevOps isn't something you *buy*. It's something you *do*."

"Look, I'm not against spending money on this if it's got a positive ROI," Jeff shot back. "That's my benchmark for every project in this building, not just IT."

"No, no, no, Jeff. You're not hearing me. DevOps isn't something you can buy, or outsource to a vendor. It's doesn't work that way. A lot of CIOs actually believe that nonsense, not Tim of course." Jonathan grinned at his old friend across the room, relishing the chance to butter him up in front of his boss.

"Well what the hell is DevOps—decipher this stuff for me you've got on the board," Jeff asked. "And how do you get DevOps?" He was at least curious enough now to ask probing questions. Jonathan's sometimes-brash style had gotten him interested in the theme.

Tim, feeling he should pitch in to show some buy-in, took the first one.

"DevOps is taking development and operations and having them work together. Instead of the two sides staying in their separate silos and only communicating when they bump up against each other, they collaborate on software programming and management. Just like the Orion marketing department has to work with corporate finance for projects to function, the two main entities in IT have to interact in a systematic way for our software—which is our main output in IT—to work."

"How do you ensure that the collaboration nets you economies of scale?" Jeff asked. "I mean, if they start crossing swords then that would just make things worse than when they were in their silos."

"Good point, Jeff" Tim offered. "The key is that they understand what they are doing to make the two sides work in sync.

For instance, we spent time today talking about how Scott and the development team would get input from Jake and security on what security features needed to be part of new applications before they are ever coded. Those features would be part of the blueprint and would get tested along the way by Ewan's operations staff. So instead of security being an abstract concept that everyone can ignore, it's something each unit has accountability for delivering."

"So the IT teams are cross-functioning?"

"Exactly. They each have their own sets of expertise, but they are all working toward a common goal."

"Wouldn't this run the risk of slowing work down, though?" Jeff asked. "Because instead of plowing away at what they do best, each IT expert has to step off the gas pedal and work a little bit outside their circle of competence, right?"

"But having common success criteria isn't an excuse for anyone to slow down. They just have to accept different outcomes. For the developers, their software may not run as fast because they've had to integrate the security features that Jake laid out for them. And in turn Jake and Ewan are going to have to accept the confines of what the developers believe they can do in terms of coding. But it's about finding an outcome that satisfies the criteria laid out in the beginning."

When Jeff still looked a bit unsold Tim decided to get more blunt.

"Jeff, you know what the key in this whole thing is so that the developers and the operations people don't bitch and moan at each other all day? Process and automation. If something is documented and automated it's not optional. You do it as part of established business procedures. Just as our district supervisors give you a very precise sales report each week or the store managers perform inventory every Sunday night, IT can have the same routine practices for deliverables. Software development is more sophisticated I'll admit, but it's not too sophisticated to be automated using the same principles that make busy restaurants operate with a high degree of order."

"Okay, I see how it works. But how do we implement it exactly?"

Jonathan intervened. "That's what we've spent most of the day doing—reorganizing each IT along DevOps principles one by one. But of course that's just an introduction, it's not a complete onboarding. So to your question, Jeff, there are really three options: you have an applications guy who takes charge, or a network guy who leads, or you hire a brand new person to command the DevOps revamp. Whoever it is commits to bridging the gap between development and operations. Ideally, it's a fresh set of eyes that adds value from the get-go by looking at the development and operations teams anew."

"Isn't that what Tim hired you for?" That was Jeff, always striving to justify every dollar, especially with labour.

"Yes—but I'm leaving tomorrow morning. I swoop in and out of places like this. I don't stay around. Even though I've taught the principles to your staff and we've even set up some automation today, that's not enough to get the job done. You need someone to take charge who can prepare Orion for ongoing DevOps. Otherwise you run the risk of going right back to the problems you had before because it hasn't sunk in with everybody in their workday lives.

"I appreciate your honesty, Jonathan," Jeff responded. "Most consultants paint themselves as the hero and don't acknowledge that they can't fix it all in one weekend. Tell us more about what kind of person we should look to bring in?"

"I'll be even more honest than that with you," Jonathan replied. "It's not easy to find a DevOps leader. Tim could do it because he understands DevOps but he's got a larger management role of running IT so he can't put a laser focus on it, which is what you need."

"Most companies just don't have that person inside the firm and they don't have somebody who can easily transition to be that person. Or they don't have a budget to bring on a new employee or a consultant. They often have to designate a makeshift DevOps leader from somewhere like development that knows about repeatability and process steps. Transitioning to a new philosophy isn't easy. It means changing the mentality of application developers taking care of the code and the systems and networking guys taking care of running the application and ne'er the twain shall meet. Like Tim was talking about before with the silo effect, there's typically in most IT departments a place where development starts and operations starts, and it's a DMZ line in between."

"So how do you undo the silo effect?" Jeff asked.

"Undoing it means starting to share knowledge and the imposition of the automation and testing methods we discussed earlier before you joined us," Jonathan said. "The DevOps leader comes into his own by commanding the automation process where the code goes from being checked in, to automatically getting updated, checked out, automatically going into operations, automatically getting rolled out and finally validated. You get what I'm saying?"

"I don't think I even know what code looks like but yeah, I think I do," Jeff replied. "It's all about leading the automation. But why couldn't one leader from either side in development or operations just do it? Couldn't that person be the one to bridge the gap to the other side and make sure automation works right since he knows how it enables the functions to fit together?"

"I see your logic in that but because all the differences in work style, attitude, and bias that have been mentioned so far really make it difficult to have a full-time developer or systems administrator be the DevOps guy," Jonathan said. "You need a role that merges the two sides into one unit. And it's not just for those subjective reasons—to ask the developer to bridge the gap when he doesn't really understand the underlying physical architecture of a network or ask the operations person to do it when they don't really understand the application, you're asking for trouble. It's just not a reasonable expectation for either one to step into this role."

"There goes my last-ditch effort to save us some money and promote in house," Jeff joked. "But seriously, then, what should we look for in a DevOps leader? Actually, Tim, what are you going to be looking for since you're the CIO who has to hire this guy?"

Tim paused before speaking to organize his thoughts since this was a critical answer to Jeff to seal the deal on convincing him of an ROI around the new position. "Well, the development background is almost a prerequisite because you're looking for somebody who understands the concept of automation, understands this concept of process, which usually developers have even if they don't realize it, because they're used to doing things in a repeatable fashion. They're used to the way they build code and the way they have to link things together.

"Whereas on the network side, you don't necessarily see those transferable skills. They can be doing things one at a time, and even though they may end up replicating some things, they're not even really thinking about it in the same perspective. So we want to find somebody who has a background in networking and systems who also is doing development, or somebody who was a developer who's now in network and systems or in security, somebody who really has worn more than the one hat."

"Jonathan, any thoughts?" Jeff asked.

"What the DevOps manager is really trying to do ultimately is blur the lines to the point that there really isn't development and operations," Jonathan said. "There's an IT team headed by Tim and they're performing a function led by this DevOps guy. Maybe he is a peacemaker but it's ultimately somebody who can play just as well or at least somewhat well on both teams. It wouldn't be hard for them to be on either side of the fence—even though their role is to eliminate that fence!"

"Do we have to do a renovation down here to put the teams side by side?" Jeff asked. "Now you've got me thinking in all sorts of directions."

"Oh you bet you do," Jonathan replied. "I've already ordered up that change from Scott and Ewan. I mean, if you had to you could keep the development and operations teams physically separate. But you're still trying to get everybody to embrace the DevOps mentality of integrated work toward an end goal. It's less about the fact that there are different teams, even if they exist, and more about the fact that you're trying to satisfy a software development life cycle. That's the roadmap for designing, building, and managing software and everybody has a role in it.

"Remember Jeff, it's not just about hiring a DevOps guy—you practice DevOps rather than purchase it—because more important is having a transition plan to DevOps. The person you hire may lead that plan, but unless everybody in your IT department buys in to the DevOps philosophy it just doesn't work because it is based on cooperation.

"If you don't get that buy-in, the application and operations teams are going to continue to fight. The developers will spew their old refrain, 'The network's slow! Your network is bogging down our application and management is pissed!' The network people will spit back, 'You've got too many lines of code and it's making too many connections! Your app is garbage.' There's this pushing back and forth because we've established these imaginary boundaries around development and operations."

"How do we stop that war then?" Jeff asked. He seemed to finally reach an appreciation for the corporate politics of IT mirroring the battles he had to referee among other divisions of the company.

"By putting them on the same team," Jonathan said. "So they no longer have to fight with each other to justify why things aren't working the way they're supposed to and it can't be their fault. They're both ultimately responsible. So if you get the DevOps philosophy embraced then if the application is not working it's now both of their faults. So they can't blame each other because from a management point of view you've embraced this whole idea of DevOps and theses groups are supporting each other, so if there's a problem the heat is on both of them."

"I like increased accountability," Jeff said. "Going back to what you said before, how do you put in a DevOps leader who is more rooted in development without pissing off operations?"

"One modern phenomenon in IT is that development in some ways is starting to act more like operations," Jonathan said. "For instance, Amazon estimates they do two to three thousand code updates *every day* for their website. From a development standpoint, Amazon's team is not building some big application and then updating it every month or quarter. It's patching it thousands of times a day to make it function continuously at a high level. Examples like this are creating a groundswell toward the idea of multiple daily code updates. That's thinking about development more from an operations point of view."

"Well, we're a decent sized company but were far from Amazon," Jeff retorted.

"It's not just for the biggest organizations; you're seeing it trickle down to smaller ones," Jonathan said. "Why? Because if you decide you have to do multiple daily updates in order to stay competitive with other applications, there's no way you could do that much updating without it being automated.

"That's why DevOps is getting so much more traction, so much more attention lately because it's forcing companies large and small to automate. They have no choice but to adopt those development principles, because it's development that's pushing the updates to them over, and over and over. Developers are coding in their own little areas and the applications are becoming much smaller."

"How can developers just code in their own little areas?" Jeff asked. "The developers here are always referencing how they lay out hundreds of thousands of lines of code in the applications they make—how do you just chop it all up like that? Wouldn't that confuse things?"

"Actually, Jeff, there's an app for that." Scott grinned ear to ear at the CEO as he said it. Tim was mortified, but took some solace in the fact that Scott had so readily internalized one of the ideas they covered that afternoon.

"Scott's right, actually," Jonathan replied. "One tool that's driving things to get smaller is Docker. It's a platform that allows you to take a big legacy application or even a smaller one and it helps you to carve all the pieces up into little chunks. Your application is like the mother ship and then you're docking all these pieces of code to the application. So you've got a bunch of developers linking up a bunch of pieces of code to hit the same model. They're all responsible for their own precisely defined areas. This automatizes the whole process into something like a manufacturing assembly line."

"Would Docker let us work with coders remotely so we're not dependent on bringing in staff here?" Jeff asked.

"Absolutely," Jonathan replied. "You want to be careful of course who you hire and they should be thoroughly vetted from afar. That's Tim and Scott's responsibility. But it's common even in the information security software world to have some developers here and some overseas.

"That means my platform is the mother ship and each one of them is building their own little components that go into it. Even though the code may work together and be doing complementary things, the developers have to compile it all into one big application. In the Docker approach, each of them could be updating their code 10 times a day or 100 times a day.

It doesn't impact the overall application, because the mother ship isn't being updated. It's just these little modules and so you're docking these modules in there."

"It really does seem to resemble a manufacturing assembly line in an esoteric way," Jeff marveled. "I mean, the computer age followed the industrial revolution so it makes sense that it would use of the best practices from it like separating duties and labour. It's the old adage, 'Everything old is new again.'"

"That's exactly right, Jeff," Jonathan said. "Today it's a great scalable way to bring a new developer in, and not have to worry about them breaking an application. I can add 10 new developers in, and they can start to contribute in different ways, and yet I'm still compartmentalizing the code. But without the DevOps platform that an application like Docker provides I wouldn't be able to follow any of those processes.

"The development people are still writing the code and the operations people are still making sure the code is working when it gets out there, but both teams rely very heavily on each other. I need to be able to get my developers' code in order to do it. And again, the less work there is in order to get the code from them to the system to roll it out, the better off they are. The same way Henry Ford found the most effective route to get the Model T down the assembly line."

"So besides the Docker concept, what are the other areas of DevOps we'll be using?" Jeff asked.

Tim thought he should take this one. He didn't want to scare

Jeff off after the Millennial meltdown. "One of the big areas DevOps is helping now is with minimum viable product," he said. "We call it MVP. It basically means you roll out the application as soon as it's viable and has the essential functions for operation. The blueprint for the product may have 20 features with 20 developers working on each individual feature but as soon as five of the features are ready to go, you can go live with those. You compartmentalize to get your MVP.

"I know that sounds risky. Especially with the word *minimum* in there. But the key to making that work from a security perspective is putting security into the MVP. We say that it doesn't work for our customers unless their personally identifiable information is secure, for instance. We make security a no compromise feature of the application, and we built it in from the beginning like we talked about earlier."

"Look, if you're going be methodical and obsessive about anything after today make it security," Jeff said. "I don't want another repeat of today, or we'll all be fired, I can tell you that. The board will just totally clean house, especially if we're a public company by then. So put all the energy and attention on security going into the product design and development, and don't go to market without it. I don't care if you go to market with the product less glitzy than it's supposed to be. I can live with that, it's our customers' data protection I can't live without."

Tim realized that this was perhaps the wisest thing said all day at Orion, even with a sage like Jonathan there. Jeff had internalized what Jonathan was imparting about security in the Software Development Life Cycle, even though he wasn't at that meeting. He understood that security was by definition part of MVP, even though MVP was a concept he'd probably just heard of for the first time today. Tim could see why someone like Jeff rose to be CEO. His background was in accounting, probably the stodgiest profession you could think of, and it made Jeff seem out of place to be the leader of a fast growing brand favored by young people. But he was a fast learner and got things immediately; not just the talking points of it but the essence of an idea. He could also apply it to day-to-day life in the company. Tim wished there were more corporate leaders like Jeff, the ones who didn't let an unfamiliarly with IT keep them from trying to solve problems.

Jonathan interjected: "You know, customers' expectations for the safety of their data, especially financial data, are so high. It's why the banks are beholden to so many rules. PayPal focused like a laser on security when they were on the frontier of Internet banking, but even they had to actually pay people to sign up at first because there was natural caution. Now the big box retailers are facing the consequences if their clients' personal identifiable information gets leaked into the wild. Orion is going to get its fair share of angry customers too. There's just basically zero tolerance for this stuff, so you have to make security ingrained in the product. We accomplish that through DevOps."

Everyone in the room seemed to be nodding their heads. For the first time all day, Tim thought, they were aware of the magnitude of the problem and how the mess with Millennial had damaged their company's reputation.

"Jonathan, let me ask you, what about the malfunctions in IT below crisis-level?" Jeff said. "How do you respond to the little fires each division in a company has to put out every day? Is there a different approach?"

"Not really," Jonathan replied. "Because DevOps offers the same benefit when it comes to troubleshooting, what you're talking about. If Orion's doing a major upgrade and it fails for some reason your development team could spend hours or days trying to isolate that within the application. If Scott uploaded his code and there was no issue, and then one of Scott's developers uploaded his code and the application crashed, I can just roll back to before that other guy uploaded his code, and the application is back up and running. That's why we obsess over version control in DevOps.

"You can quickly isolate it so that failures like release failures are much lower, there's a much smaller incidence of them and you can respond to them and can resolve them a lot quicker than you could during a rollout."

"I can't believe we weren't already doing this," Jeff exclaimed.

"You're not a small company so you definitely should," Jonathan replied with a chuckle." I mean, there's no way Amazon could get by without doing this kind of automation. When you consider the volume of updates they do, there's no way they could do this manually. They wouldn't be able to keep up with it or keep track of it. So automation is the underpinning of DevOps."

"There's even a way for them to help you. Amazon has a system called Apollo available for their cloud customers. It's built into Amazon Web Services for companies to be able to use to do their automated software deploys. So if you're doing your development in an AWS environment or you're running a cloud platform in the AWS environment you can take advantage of Code Deploy, that same engine that they use, and use it to roll code at once or a million times, whatever the volume is. There are many other products that have come out on the market that are all designed for software code deployment. They're all trying to satisfy that DevOps philosophy."

"Well, if it's from Amazon it's got to be a good deal!" Jeff exclaimed.

"You've got to be careful with automated code deployment," Jonathan cautioned. "Yes, the application is going to become more effective, but you will also have a higher probability of introducing more security problems in this type of an approach because of the automation. If you're doing thousands of rollouts a day how could you possibly be testing the application as thoroughly as I could be if you did one rollout and a full vulnerability assessment against the application?"

"Sure, I get it," Jeff said.

"What that means is it requires far more rigor for security at the developer's side in the code they're building," Jonathan continued. "They have to be doing their own regression testing to weed out the vulnerabilities in their code. Regression testing is primarily used for evaluating functionality—you regress your updated version against the last version of the application and see if it works right. But that scientific process is used to isolate security vulnerabilities the same way."

"Who's it going to be more work for?" Jeff asked. "By that I mean, who's going to be complaining to Tim the most when we start with DevOps?" He shot Tim a wry grin.

"In the beginning, DevOps is more work for the developers," Jonathan replied. "It means they'll leave a bit less time for coding, they're going to have to spend more time explaining and working towards that coding application and coding automation scripts. So they've got to understand what the bigger picture is. For the operations people, it's the same thing. They've typically never been involved in coding before. So they're going to have to learn some scripting and other new things. There are automated frameworks like Chef and Puppet that can help with that. Some people on the IT team will embrace that and think it's a great opportunity, and then you may have lifers or careerists who say, 'I never had to write a script before. Why the hell should I start writing a script now?' or, 'I don't have a clue how to write code. That's just not my strength.' Or just simply, 'I hate change.'"

"We don't have any of those people down here do we?" Jeff mused aloud.

Tim thought back to earlier in the day when it was clear that, *yes we do*. No one fit the definition of a careerist better than Glenn on the server side. Ewan could be called the same, having advanced up to his position through the Peter

Principle—though his problem was less in his attitude than his competence. Jake was simply powerless, and might as well have not even been a part of the company. Scott was like a younger version of Glenn, a know-it-all fiercely protective of his silo. If anyone had been given a team of DevOps naysayers, it was Tim.

But that was *then*. The long day of instruction—no, evangelism—from Jonathan had caused cracks in their armor until it finally came off, Tim thought. He made them recognize that their own ways of doing things weren't working. Deep down, they weren't happy because their work wasn't effective; only their silos were. They could leave at the end of the day with their heads held high because they owned their turf, never because Orion's IT infrastructure worked like it should. They didn't bring out the best in one another because they didn't work together. Jonathan' pulled the wool up from over their eyes and made a group of recalcitrant employees see another way. Their buy-in to DevOps rested on the deal that cross functioning was critical to making IT function like it should. It took the catastrophe of their new application crashing and burning followed by Jonathan's intervention to get them there, but now they were practically totally unrecognizable as a unit from just one day earlier.

For each unit there will be new things to learn and different types of work to do because DevOps is going to impact them in some way while they put the system processes in place. But the reward would be freeing up a massive amount of time for them, so that the developers can code much faster and the operations people has fewer breakdowns to deal with.

They can get the product to market faster and everyone is happy, including management. As Tim saw it, giving up some autonomy for this free time was a great tradeoff to everyone, including upstairs at the C-level.

"Jonathan, could you talk about automation a little more?" Tim asked. "I want to make sure we lay out the benefits and challenges of automation because it's such a key thing you do within DevOps. Like you said, there are risks involved when you automate at great speed or load."

"That's right," Jonathan replied. "With DevOps the tools do most of the work. That's the reward for setting up those tools and living with the rules of the road for them. But you have to follow this rule when you set up those tools to do the automation: Don't automate what you don't understand. To me it's kind of like when I visit a big city and rent a car—I don't just start driving the freeways and mixing it up with the local commuters because I don't want to battle traffic I don't understand. Until you really understand from beginning to end where is it coming from, where is it going to, what are the things that are being affected by the change, why are we making this change, how often, all those things, then you risk causing more problems with automation. Because it will just keep on running and there will be more fires to put out. You have to make sure to put in checks and balances that will prevent automation from getting out of control and losing any human input.

"In my consulting practice, we might do something once, twice, 20 times, a 100 times, manually. Here at Orion you might have Jake run the malware detection tool manually to really clearly understand exactly what the threats are he's looking for. Only once he has worked all the kinks out and figured out how to best set up and run the software does he stop doing it manually. When the security people or the developers or the operations guys or whoever have got the guts of the program you are ready to let it fly."

"See how two teams working together comes in handy?" Tim said to the group, eying Jake and Ewan and Glenn and Scott from side to side. "If some security intrusion happens with an application and Jake doesn't understand what's wrong, Ewan doesn't understand, well then Scott or someone on his team can explain it and vice-versa. So whoever it is being instructed about the intrusion doesn't need Scott to teach it to him a hundred times; if he's taught those first few times then at least he and his DevOps team can start to really understand collectively what does this automated process to repel and seal the intrusion needs to look like, how it needs to work, and what they need to feed into it and get out of it. You're not just dealing with the process; you're dealing with the information in it."

"Glad you used the intrusion example, since that's why we're all here anyway," Jonathan said. "Automation is also a big step in securing a company's information technology. Doing that makes you build out some type of framework to understand security, what is it you're actually *supposed* to be doing. Then you develop a set of requirements for it. You build control points, or tasks, or things that you're going to do to order to satisfy those requirements and then put stuff in place in order to measure or validate, to make sure you're doing those things.

It's the tasks that you can really automate the hell out of."

"Jonathan, I'm following you but can you be a little more specific?" Jeff asked. What is the type of task you would automate the hell out of?"

Tim admired Jeff's willingness to ask simple, direct questions across areas he knew nothing or very little about. As CEO he didn't pretend to know more than anyone else in each leader's own department, but he sure knew the best questions to ask in each discipline. That meant he was getting the best information possible. The same could be said about Jonathan—he assuredly didn't know how to code as elegantly as Scott or know the world of servers as well as Glenn, but he sure knew how to fix their work operations by asking them the right questions to figure out what was wrong and how to fix it.

"Well Jeff, checking for bugs could be one thing you automate," Jonathan replied. "Consider software deployment in the traditional way that software developers do their work: they get their code down to a search point. They may be compiling it themselves or maybe a runtime compiler. They've got to put that code somewhere, so they put in a library, they've got it all registered and done. And then somehow that has to get to the operations team who in turn has to get it into production and get it all up and operational. That's the legacy approach, and it's a manual process.

"Automating that would be every time your software developer uploads his code to the source code repository, there's an automated process that kicks that off, checks, and validates it and makes sure that the code he put in meets a certain criteria. Once it takes his code in it automatically rolls it out, then it automatically runs these 32 tests or whatever the arbitrary number is and as long as 29 of those 32 tests pass or whatever the criterion is, then we're comfortable with that software being live and in production."

"Tim, was Millennial's software deployment done the first way, the manual way?" Jeff asked.

"Yes, Jeff, and to be fair to our development team, most code deployment today is being done by a person," Tim answered. "And the challenge we have is with measuring and validating once the deployment is complete. Without automation that's the part that almost never gets done, because we may automate the process, but the checking and validating, if we're still relying on a person to do all of it, it's inevitable somebody's unavailable at some point. It could be the day that we're scheduled to update the software—Code Tuesday—and the person who does that every Tuesday is sick or on vacation. So they can't do it.

"Automating all of that testing and validation takes the human element out of the equation and allows us to have that whole automated process run that same way every time because we're not relying on a person to be a crucial component anymore."

"I like people, but I love the idea of taking the human out of it," Jeff said in his faint Texas drawl to laughs all around.

After taking a three-minute coffee break, the group reassembled around the conference table. Jeff spoke first.

"You know, all this time I've still been worried about it happening again. Orion gets hacked somehow. Maybe it's our employees' information like our payroll data. Or maybe its proprietary marketing intelligence that some other restaurant company would like to get their hands on. You never know right? So I just want to know what the protocol is if God forbid we get hit again, even if it's not on the scale of what hit us yesterday."

"That's exactly the mindset you should be in, Jeff," Jonathan responded. "Because I can't guarantee you invincibility from cyber intrusion. DevOps can't either. You have to have a response plan in place. That's part of DevOps itself.

"There are typically three places where you will get notified of a breach. It's coming from an alert, with the system saying, 'Hey, I'm seeing this type of behavior,' and that behavior is an indicator of a compromise. Or it's coming from a user who is calling and saying, 'Hey, look at this!' It could be an internal user or an outside customer reporting something strange and tipping you off about it. Or finally it could be a third party calling you to say, 'We're seeing your credit card information out there.' Like what happened yesterday when Tim got woken up at 5 in the morning yesterday. But it could also come from a vendor or another firm you do business with.

"You always want to hear about it the first way from your systems," Jonathan continued, "because if you hear about it from your systems then the odds are good that you can fix it, stop it, change it, do whatever before your users are impacted. So it comes down to making your systems hardened. Are the tools functioning? Are they set up to look for the vulnerabilities the security team tried to address before they were installed? Just like how in DevOps we meticulously integrate security into homegrown applications, the security tools we use have to be calibrated with the same kind of attention to detail."

"I don't just worry about the ramifications of us getting attacked again on our customers or employees," Jeff continued. "I worry about its impact on our reputation. Word is going to get out about this one with Millennial and the thirty thousand customers whose information was compromised. Of course, and if we have another hit, even if it's not as big, it's going to seriously undermine the reputation of Orion to do business, even in our core competency of selling burgers and beers. I don't want us to be the next Target!"

"Target had a 12 percent sales decline in the month following the breach, which happened to be December during the holiday shopping season," Jonathan said. "It wasn't that they all of a sudden couldn't process credit cards or keep the inventory flowing; customers just didn't trust it as much. So you're right, Jeff, the reputational risk is huge."

"We couldn't survive that kind of loss in same-store sales our busiest time of the year during football season," Jeff said. "As a growing, almost public market company we'd be written off. The whole story would be, 'Look at how they're collapsing!' So I want to make it our mission here in IT to make sure that doesn't happen."

"Then let's talk paying for it—and I don't just mean in dollars," Jonathan said. He seemed eager to close the sale of DevOps to Jeff, which meant getting him to foot the bill for it too. Tim admired Jonathan for this; he didn't sugarcoat the costs involved and leave them for the company to sort out after he left. He wasn't going to rev up their CEO and then let the air deflate out of the balloon later on when there had to be a difficult meeting of explaining the tradeoffs.

"Companies are inclined to underinvest in security systems because there are costs associated with them. Going back to the picture of a typical information security guy, they want to install layers and layers of defenses. All these layers have costs, whether it's a people cost, whether it's a resource cost of getting things setup, whether it's a technology cost. So budgets come into play.

"On the budget side for DevOps, there are really three primary things that people look at when building software. There's the dollar budget, there's the people budget and there's the time budget. If any of those things are impacted it's inevitable that the deliverable product is going to be impacted."

"Well what is it we're going to let slip?" Jeff asked, looking mostly at Tim and Scott. "Does it take longer to get done? Do you need more people to be able to get it in the same timeframe? I hate missing deadlines so I don't want us to pay the cost in time."

"Yes—we'll need more people," Tim answered. "The most immutable thing in software is always time. The marketing or finance people that are asking for the application never want to sacrifice it, usually because they've made some public release date to our customers or employees. With Millennial, there was never a question of slowing down its development because the ad time had been bought in advance; the stores were getting fitted for the rollout. I get that, and there's nothing here in IT that we can or should do to change it. But all I ask is that we get enough manpower ahead of time to fit the application's development schedule and due date."

"Jeff, I'm not going to kid you," Jonathan said. "If Tim doesn't have the budget to sufficiently fund a project and you've made a commitment to your customers about having this product to market by a certain date, functionality is most in play to be sacrificed. You can either hire more developers, which if the date's not that far away isn't going to help much anyway because of the learning curve involved, or scale back the application. So it's almost inevitable that typically what gets sacrificed is features or functionality.

"That's not necessarily a bad thing," he continued. "We see that all the time when Microsoft rolls out a new version, and all along they were talking about it was going to have something specific, and then when it first gets released it doesn't have that thing and then it's there in Service Pack 1. So they've taken those features out and said, 'We're just going with what was built on time, we'll include that feature with the next update to the software.' Nobody cries over it."

"So they just keep updating rather than wait and then include those features in the next generation of the program?" Jeff asked.

"That's the beauty of the software as a service (SaaS) or cloud model, whichever you want to call it," Jonathan said. "As soon as you have that new feature or function available you put it in the software when it's ready. You don't have to wait for a cycle or anything like that. It could be tomorrow. It could be three weeks from now. You could just add it in right away and everybody gets to take advantage of it because the application is accessed online rather than through an internal network or software."

"We talked earlier today about MVP—the minimum viable product," Tim said. "SaaS encourages you to go with the MVP and then keep updating it to get it better. So there's less pressure on that release date and more emphasis on getting the product right rather than just finishing it, like we did with Millennial."

"Why don't more companies refrain from setting public deadlines for their new products given the risk that they will struggle to meet them?" Jeff asked. "I mean, our marketing people fell into that trap hook, line, and sinker with Millennial. But Apple never gives a hard date for their new iPhone or iPad. They announce an event with only a few weeks' notice and then unveil the product there. They never seem to lack any buzz or excitement. We got desperate and bought into the idea that the interest hinged on some arbitrary date."

"You're highlighting a weakness nobody talks about, Jeff," Jonathan said. "For most product companies, the problem is that their current product really isn't wowing the industry and when they're building a new version they want the hype to be out there around it. They also need to keep their share price up as much as they possibly can, or deal with the fact that a competitor has brought in a new product that's just as good if not better. So they use traditional marketing strategy of built-in anticipation and a press calendar to obsess over the delivery date.

"Another factor that heightens the sense of urgency for delivery is that brand loyalty to companies has dropped significantly. It's not that difficult anymore to switch from Company A, to Company B, to Company C, to Company Z anymore. It's nowhere near as difficult as it used to be. The ease of use in software as a service enables low switching costs. At least you only have to make software at Orion for yourself, not the cutthroat B2B market!"

"I think we better stick to burgers," Jeff joked. "But seriously, I can't be the only one upstairs believing in DevOps. The same marketing people who were a thorn in the side of you guys down here during Millennial's development have to be squared away. So does finance and human resources—because they'll have to appropriate the funding and adopt the new org chart for this to work. Even my own board of directors has to be tied in for something this far-reaching."

"Jeff, let me propose something to you that I have yet to pitch to a company," Jonathan said. "I think Orion should establish a standing committee for information technology on its board of directors. The committee would oversee IT practices, investment, and security parameters. It wouldn't interfere with Tim's mission to run the department, but give him input and serve as a sort of ombudsman for IT in the company.

Boards already grapple with the complex corporate issues—the accounting, the executive compensation, regulation, etc.—why not IT? It's just as important as anything else, and with consumer-facing companies like Orion so reliant on technology their operations and reputation depend on it working. It's time to formalize this in your corporate governance."

Tim remembered Jonathan bringing up this idea with him over the phone about two years ago, when he was in his last company, the consulting firm. At the time it hadn't made much of an impression on him. There were lots of problems with corporate boards already and adding an offshoot to oversee IT was a risky proposition. But in the intervening time, having seen how far removed corporate leaders were from IT and how it was hurtling at them like a freight train—the credit card theft at Target, the multiple Sony hackings, the health insurers seeing their patient's medical-related personal identifiable information being swiped—he became convinced that it was reckless for corporate boards not to address IT in an ongoing way just like they do other headline issues.

In Tim's mind, the biggest benefit from a standing IT committee on the board was that it would put pressure on companies to elevate people with IT backgrounds to their leadership. No longer would experts in security, operations, or development be consigned to overseeing firms only within those business spaces; instead companies in a wide range of categories would look to those people for leadership because they needed their expertise in their corporate governance. Under this model, it was entirely plausible for Exxon Mobil to include an information security pioneer on their board or Starbucks to tap an

IT operations star. IT leaders would cross-pollinate across a number of industries to emphasize its importance.

Would Jeff be up for another board committee that would eventually require him to find new candidates to help fill it? The company's plan was to go public relatively soon, and a change in corporate governance might be looked at as a red flag. Plus, was there even anyone on the board qualified to serve on that type of committee?

"You know, quite honestly I'm not satisfied with the board I have right now," Jeff said. That was a candid admission from a CEO. "They don't take an interest in specific workings of the company and get under the hood. Most of the meets are pretty regimented and have a pro forma feel. It's been my goal to get the board engaged, and I think adding an IT responsibility to it in the aftermath of this breach is a way to do that.

"I don't want this to be a cover-your-ass move where we point to a committee of the board and say 'There's our IT security supervision—so we should pass the audit.' Whoever we have on it has to provide real input and supervision on DevOps and any other IT reform we undertake. It will probably mean finding additional board members to handle these responsibilities. I'm fine with that, because I now believe the benefits as you all have shown me surely outweigh the costs."

Tim could hardly believe this was the same Jeff talking. Just the day before on the onset of the Millennial catastrophe he had been reluctant to even retain Jonathan because of the costs. His move toward quenching the crisis was hearing from some public relations blowhard. Now Orion's CEO was immersed in a planning meeting about DevOps and having in-depth conversations about security testing and product launches. He approved on the spot a new committee of the board dedicated to IT. Tim marveled about the teaching and evangelism from Jonathan that had persuaded Jeff to move from stereotypical disconnected CEO to DevOps convert that weekend.

"Jonathan," Tim interjected. "You know, everyone at this company who is going to have to buy into DevOps isn't here at this meeting. Not just the board members but demanding company division managers who interface with IT." He thought of Alex from marketing. "So how do we convince our colleagues and corporate leaders to spend on DevOps, especially if they're in a field not directly tied to technology?"

"Well," Jonathan answered. 'There are a couple different ways. One way is to have an evangelist on site to talk about what the benefit is going to be. It could be a consultant like me, or someone who comes on fulltime to lead DevOps. So look for that messaging skill in the person you hire to lead DevOps here. That person needs to have a strong enough personality when it comes to pitching the concept of DevOps to break through all the IT investment preconceptions—it's a waste of money, it's too confusing—so that there's a real teaching opportunity there, at least for the basics.

"This evangelist should be able to show a cost benefit analysis for DevOps investment just like Jeff alluded to earlier," Jonathan continued." You may spend this much money in automation and processes but on the backend here's how much time you can save on average per month. If you're doing one rollout a quarter versus one rollout per day, here's the upfront cost it may take you to get the DevOps philosophy embedded, but then here's the dollars that you can save down the road. So there's the return on investment."

"ROI," Jeff said aloud. "It's the H-bomb of corporate politics."

"What do you mean?" Scott asked.

"Everything we do at a company like this draws some kind of opposition from somewhere," Jeff said. "It's particularly potent opposition for you guys down here in IT because no one really understands what you do, so they don't appreciate it. Whether its restaurant operations pissed off with something human resources has done or marketing unhappy with how the finance department is handling their funds, there's always a kerfuffle at the place where change happens.

"The only surefire way to stop it and shut up the naysayers is to prove the ROI. Because if the company is coming out ahead with the new practice or policy in place, how can anyone seriously oppose it? Just because they don't like it or it's annoying? Those are baseless attacks. I still hear them made, but they don't get you very far in serious discussion. It's Orion's corporate mission to maximize the return on our shareholders' investment, which will become the expectation of the marketplace when we go public. So I always tell our managers, if you want to win the day with your argument for change, show me and everyone else the ROI."

"That's exactly what we're doing with DevOps, Jeff," Tim said. He was thrilled to hear his boss extrapolate a CEO principle to what they were doing in remaking the IT department. DevOps is about being effective and efficient, about getting more done at less cost—in both dollar and man-hour terms. Jeff seemed to now get this intuitively. No generic corporate retreat could have produced as much understanding as flying in Jonathan and cramming on DevOps, Tim thought to himself. It was the best two days of work he'd had in a long time, even though it fell on a weekend and was precipitated by a catastrophe.

The intensity in the room dissipated as finally no one had anything to follow up with. They appeared mentally spent. Tim thought of something an old boss had said when readying for a big work trip, that he would rather be fully prepared and tired rather than underprepared and fresh. That was how everyone around the table looked now, and it was satisfying. They were worn out but far from tense, even at peace. He looked at his watch and realized that it was late enough, even on a Saturday night, his family would all be in bed by now.

"Gentlemen, I suggest we proceed to the bar up the street and have a round to decompress," Tim said. "I want to thank you for putting in long hours this weekend and your willingness to adopt a new approach to your work. Drinks are on me."

He had looked more in the direction of Scott, Ewan and Jake when he said this, not expecting Jeff to be interested in continuing a long evening by unwinding with his staff. "Nope, drinks are on *me*," Jeff said. "Consider it the first expense item on the DevOps revamp."

The others looked at one another quizzically, not sure what to make of this pronouncement. Jeff continued: "Ha, just kidding—that would be Jonathan's consulting fee. And I'm buying the drinks personally. Let's not get carried away here!"

With the confusion settled, the group barged out of the office building and into the night, embracing a group plan that had eluded Orion's information technology unit until that moment of crisis put in motion the call to make things work in cohesion. Thanks to DevOps, they were cutting a path to effectiveness in IT. Even with their mess of a mobile app still to clean up, everyone had a reason to feel good about their future within the organization.

BREACHED! STUDY GUIDE

Introduction

I. *The dreaded 5 a.m. phone call—CIO is awoken by law enforcement authorities and informed of likely cyber breach involving tens of thousands of individuals*

1. What is it? Breach of new mobile payment application

2. What impact is it having? Theft of personal identifiable information

3. What are we going to do to fix it? To be determined

II. *How CIO got here*

1. Hired as burger restaurant chain's first CIO just two weeks prior after previous stints in network and operations at software firm—this is his first

consumer oriented company and first time as leader of IT department

2. Position had appeal because of growth trend of Company (likely to go public soon) and its willingness to spend on IT systems like point of service technology

3. Company has 2,400 employees—mostly hourly restaurant workers—and modest-sized corporate headquarters with IT installed in basement of building

III. Project Millennial

1. Point of sale mobile app aimed at younger customer base

2. Usage expected to be heavy upon debut owing to brand's large email list and social media following

3. Deadline to ship is two weeks after CIO's arrival

4. Marketing department is leading charge to keep hard deadline intact despite development overload and lack of security integration along the way

5. CIO reconnects with old friend IT Consultant a week before Millennial launch, who gives him stern warning that mobile app likely has inadequate security after being rushed to shipment

IV. C-Level Meeting

1. CIO convenes conference call of CEO, COO, CMO, and Communications VP

2. Communications VP tries to deflect blame from Company; says it could be vendor

3. CEO accepts law enforcement's suspicion that Company is at fault; orders executives to reconvene at headquarters as soon as possible

4. CIO decides to call IT Consultant for help since his warning came true

V. Headquarters

1. Consultant agrees over phone to fly in to assess damage and fix IT department

2. CIO must persuade CEO to hire IT Consultant and give him authority to overhaul IT

3. Meanwhile, Crisis Consultant is commanding C-level executives' attention and shaping catastrophe through lens of public relations and media

VI. CEO Persuasion

1. CIO makes case to CEO that fixing IT needs to be focus, not public relations

2. CEO doesn't want to do IT revamp because of money and timing

3. CIO persuades CEO that revamping organized by IT Consultant will save money and fix mess created by Millennial in first place

Creating a Plan with CEO and IT Consultant

I. *Staff meeting*

1. CIO convenes leaders of each IT unit to coordinate response to breach

2. Network/systems lead wants to replace server

3. Operations manager can't see into systems and determine whom he should lock out; also does not want to shut down all systems and close down business

4. Applications chief rejects idea that code was vulnerable and wants to go into logging to see where intrusion occurred

5. Argument breaks out between operations and applications leaders

6. Meeting ends with department in chaos and each manager going their separate ways on reaction to breach

II. *Enter IT Consultant*

1. IT Consultant gives CIO overview of security vulnerabilities on ride from airport

2. Software Development Life Cycle—supposed to streamline software-making but security often gets sidelined

3. Security has to get "bolted on" at end

4. Developers aren't taught security in school and security guys aren't working with developers upon building software

5. Testing is critical: static testing against source code and dynamic testing against live application

6. Standard imaging can leave common vulnerabilities across servers and computers—therefore it must be tested so the system is hardened against threats

7. New gold image for operating system should be made each time patching is done

8. Security updates are different than other software updates: they are less likely to be acted on because IT departments tend to update gold images after lots of patches

9. Treat patching like you're creating a new gold image, because that's what you're doing

10. Network rules like firewalls are critical to security but often get bypassed in favor of performance

11. Layers of security add latency—how much is company willing to deal with?

12. Regular internal audits are superior to typical annual external audit—it's like seeing dentist regularly to keep teeth cleaned rather than waiting for plaque to build up

13. Regular audit is real-time picture of IT; annual audit is just snapshot

14. Security tools need to be calibrated in order to work, including plumbing, rules, alerts and updates

Information Security Person

I. Profile

1. CIO barely heard from him in first two weeks on job

2. Managed service provider used for information security

3. "Everyone seems to walk all over him"—he signed off on bolted on security for Millennial app before product was shipped

II. Intervention by Consultant

1. Consultant and Information Security Person have animated conversation behind closed doors, which leads to a consensus

2. Information Security Person is actually powerless because company doesn't care about security; it's just a box to check

3. Managed service provider being used to avoid any security interference with operations

4. Only way he could garner respect was establishing security silo and pretending he was essential

5. Developers convinced Information Security Person to sign off on SDLC that had static coding at end, right before application went live

6. Information Security Person buys into Consultant's ideas about regular patching and tool usage so that he can become empowered within Company IT

Operations Manager

I. Profile

1. Served in same role at rival restaurant company

2. Seen as safe pick because his credentials said he was qualified

3. Yet routine tasks like patching and hardware replacement weren't getting done

II. *Intervention by Consultant*

1. Operations Manager has no idea where breach happened

2. Plumbing done by operations group on security tool is like plumbing done on router or switch

3. Had no idea how application was supposed to work

4. In defensive mode, brought managed security provider to investigate application

5. No Business Continuity Plan exists—Company needs rules of road for shutting down business systems in event of intrusion

6. Plan should include shutting systems down, disconnecting from Internet, disconnecting from network, and bringing systems back online

7. Everything needs to be documented during intrusion investigation in case company has to go to court

8. CIO's challenge is to eliminate wall between security and operations and get them to collaborate

9. Testing and patching are the most effective things to automate

10. Operations Manager buys into Consultant's pitch to work with Information Security so that operations can work in a more regimented, functional manner and can be integrated with rest of IT

Network/Systems Person

I. *Profile*

1. Responsible for client-server architecture and executing tasks like web, mail, printing, remote file access, and proprietary applications and databases

2. Has longest tenure of anyone in IT that enabled him to build moat around role

3. CIO views him as most arrogant manager in IT department; he is personification of silo system

II. *Intervention by Consultant*

1. Network/Systems Person has replaced server without consulting with CIO or anyone else; he claims Millennial application is now functioning properly

2. Original server for application is gone but hole found by intruders is still there—the vulnerability still exists and will be exploited if application is turned back on

3. Back-to-back break-ins happen all the time; hackers are persistent

4. Systems team should do vulnerability assessment against every new server to make sure they find vulnerabilities and patch them

5. Test application once it's deployed for application-specific vulnerabilities

6. Company would have been better off taking server offline to do security scan and keeping the application down rather than trying to get it live again as soon as possible like Network/Systems Person wants

7. Must take image of server before it's blown away to do forensics investigation

8. Server Deployment Life Cycle: build book tells you how to build, stage, deploy, and test and run book tells you how to operate and maintain a server

9. Information Security Person needs to be check on Network/Systems Person on making sure build and run books are exhaustive and all security-related aspects are injected

10. Server Deployment Life Cycle needs to be strict and regimented so that when new employees come on board the don't deviate or use their own practices

11. Knowledge has to be transferrable rather than bottled up in one employee or silo

12. Network/Systems Person is convinced to change approach from silo to integration with security and rest of IT with argument from Consultant that his expertise will be more valuable when it's enshrined in processes, procedures, and task that everyone will follow rather than continuing to be applied in ad hoc way

Application Person

I. Profile

1. Most isolated and autonomous of any manager under CIO's authority

2. Was ally of Chief Marketing Officer, who pushed hard for Millennial's delivery

3. Had no previous experience as development manager or integrating his products with security and operational features that Company size demanded

II. Intervention by Consultant

1. Application Person is best positioned to fix problem because he has most relevant knowledge of where the breach is targeting

2. Development is isolated from Operations just like vice-versa; most companies don't let development people touch production aspects

3. Workflow between Development and Operations should emulate the automated manufacturing line rather crude and disjointed handoffs

4. Cross-functioning is critical skill in DevOps: working together in automated process to roll out application in consistent, reliable, repeatable fashion

5. First step in enabling cross-functioning is getting teams to physically sit near each other, second step is finding consensus on Software Development Life Cycle

6. Software Development Life Cycle is build book for software

7. Since security must be baked in Software Development Life Cycle, developers need to learn secure coding principles like using parameters for fields

8. Bad code reuse is epidemic in software development

9. Session persistence, session fixation, session crossover and session reuse are specific entry-point vulnerabilities familiar to security people but not developers—but they must be dealt with by developers with coding practices like randomized sessions

10. Version control lets developers have a central

repository of changes so code can be “checked in” and “checked out”

11. Functional specifications by the business-side people are followed by technical specifications by the developers—only once those are finished should anyone start coding

12. Waterfall is traditional approach to development: everything is methodically planned out

13. Agile is newer and more cutting edge approach to development that prioritizes effectiveness over symmetry to build a Minimum Viable Product (MVP)

14. MVP is defined as what an application needs to be at a basic minimum in order it for it to be sold or provided to end users

15. Sprint is process in agile development of prioritizing and concentrating on building chosen functions to maximize effectiveness

16. Scrum meetings are held during sprints to chart progress and plan work

17. Complication with agile approach is remaining functions don’t get planned out: sometimes code has to be thrown out as new functions are added and security has to be added along the way rather than planned in advance like in waterfall approach

18. Code notation is vital to developers working together in harmony so they can understand and track each other's work; this helps with employee turnover

19. Time, features, and budget are three constraints of software development and the challenge for security is to integrate it through the pressure of these constraints

20. Risks of bolting on security instead of integrating it are that it can be knocked right off or worked around by intruders

21. Application Person is persuaded of changes because products will be more credible and burden of providing security for software would be shared with Information Security Person

All About DevOps

1. CEO stipulates positive return on investment as his criterion for DevOps, just like any other corporate program

2. DevOps isn't something you buy—it's something you do

3. Just like marketing has to work with finance, development and operations should work together in IT

4. Each unit uses their specific expertise to work toward common IT goal

5. Company commits to hiring DevOps leader: could be developer, network guy, or outside person

6. CIO is commissioned to hire outside person to fulfill role—looking for someone who understands automation and process, making it more likely that he will pick person with development background rather than network background

7. Development is starting to act more like operations in modern IT—e.g. Amazon ships thousands of code updates every day

8. Programming assignments can be dispersed and then code can be attached to application via Docker tool to resemble a manufacturing line

9. Minimum Viable Product understood by CEO to prioritize security over glitz

10. Automatic code deployment is core of DevOps but since updates will be so much heavier in volume security testing needs to be ratcheted up in corresponding fashion

11. Sacrifice of learning new skills was rewarded by free time created by reduction of malfunctions in DevOps

12. Software as a service enables firms to release updates as they are finished, rather than wait for

next generation and deal with pressure of release dates

13. Apple is good example of brand that eschews long-running release buildup and yet still generates public excitement and media interest around their products

14. Consultant proposes committee on IT for Company's board of directors

15. CEO is persuaded because IT is complex issue that deserves board's attention the way finance, regulation, and other business practices do

16. Committee would also put pressure on firms to elevate people with IT skills and knowledge to their leadership—IT people could cross-pollinate across industries

17. Bringing in DevOps evangelist is good way to onboard employees to concept

CHECKLIST FOR YOUR BUSINESS: MAKING IT SECURE AND EFFECTIVE

Are you ready to implement the improvements and recommendations contained in *Breached!* in your business? Here is a checklist to help you get started:

- **Validation metrics**: determine the quantitative outcomes needed to justify IT investment so that they produce a return on investment

- **Reporting metrics**: organize into dashboard the key IT functions that can provide real-time data, e.g. intrusion threats

- **Software Development Life Cycle**: compose build and run books for programming and operating software according to agreed upon rules and practice from development and operations

- **Operations Life Cycle**: build books and run books for staging and operating server—automate server practices like software development

- **Standard imaging**: harden for security threats by rereleasing every time there is a security patch so that no machine or server is outdated

- **Network architecture**: make sure traffic is not rerouted around firewalls or other tools on the network without assessing the impact on security

- **Audits**: conduct regular (monthly, quarterly) audits from independent firm (not the same vendor providing managed security service) rather than the annual audit typically required to remain complaint with industry regulation

- **Scripts**: use scripts to check for breaches rather than relying on employees to maintain scrutiny; this requires central repository of rules

- **Tool management**: assign responsible to person for making sure tool is doing what it is supposed to do and have person calibrate automation so tool runs properly without need for human involvement

- **Effective investigation**: when security threat is found, learn to ask the right questions to solve problem: 1) What is it? 2) What's the impact? 3) What are we supposed to do about it?

- **Patching**: security tools and other programs should be patched as updates become available; don't wait to update in bulk or systems will be vulnerable during those periods

- **Documentation**: important to reduce reliance on individual employees and to create practices for integrating development and operations (e.g. Software Development Life Cycle); also critical during security meltdown should company ever need to go to court

- **Version control**: separate and organize versions of applications so that programmers can work autonomously and keep track of changes without any confusion

BUILDING AN EFFECTIVE INFORMATION SECURITY PROGRAM

Initial Gap Analysis

Perform an initial gap analysis, to try to determine where you are vs where you want to be. If you have any standards you are trying to be compliant to, use them to measure yourself against, as well as any existing corporate information security policies. ISO 27001 is an effective framework to use when measuring information security preparedness and should be incorporated into your planning.

Vulnerability Assessment

Perform (or hire a third party to perform) a vulnerability assessment against your internal and external network hosts. This will give you insights into the current security exposures your organization may already have, and also helps you to establish a baseline to work against to improve your overall information security posture while at the same time aligning the findings with those from the gap analysis above.

Perform Analysis, Determine Current Risk Exposures

Once you have both sets of information, combine it all together to gain a basic understanding of where you are now vs where you want to be. The findings you identify here should be action items that you can address either immediately to remediate the problem, such as identified vulnerabilities, or may require only be addressed during the creation of a requirement along with control objectives when building out your framework in the next step.

Create a Framework, Perform a Maturity Model Rating

Using any regulatory requirements, along with ISO 27001 and optionally frameworks like the SANS CSC (Critical Security Controls), build out a policy framework that identifies things you should be doing, and talks about how you should be doing them. You should then perform a maturity rating against each item to understand how far along you are on each item, or whether they are even started.

Build a Roadmap

Once your framework is complete, build out a roadmap addressing each item in your framework. The goal of the roadmap is to identify potential costs to implement each item, amount of effort required to implement, potential resources required, and any timelines and timeframes. Finally you should prioritize each item in the roadmap to help make a final determination of what should be tackled and when.

Depending on the size and complexity of your roadmap, you should plan on it taking anywhere from 1-3 years to accomplish all your roadmap tasks.

Maintaining Compliance, Measuring Success

One of the most overlooked steps when building out an information security program is remembering to build in validation activities and ways to track and measure progress. For your over-arching information security program, you should identify a maximum of 5 key goals for the program. These can be measured using a streetlight analogy, and are useful when reporting to senior management or to a Board of Directors. All of the requirements and objectives identified in your framework should align to one of these 5 items. Build out a scorecard that allows you to measure all of the items in your framework, and aggregate the results to in turn set the final result for each of your key program goals. In order to measure each item, you need to create a validation process or method for each item in the framework. This will tell you how to measure each item, ideally identify who should be performing the activity, how often they should be performing the validation, and what success means for each item.

Attain and Maintain

By following all of the activities outlined above, and in order, you can implement an incredibly effective information security program, allowing you to determine what your risk posture looks like today, what changes you need to make to improve your risk posture tomorrow, and ultimately what you need to be checking and validating on an ongoing, repeatable basis to ensure you don't just get compliant, but stay compliant!

GLOSSARY

Attain and maintain

Once a company gets compliant, there's a real tendency to assume things are complete. This couldn't be further from the truth. The spirit of the compliance activities is to get the organization to accomplish goals with a particular purpose; in the case of information security, it's to improve your security posture and reduce your overall risk exposure. Once you get compliant, it's imperative that you continue to test and validate the activities you took in order to get, there, hence the term "attain and maintain," or "get there and stay there."

Agile development

In Agile development, the requirements and solutions for software development evolve during the development process itself. A basic set of criteria is defined and then development commences relatively early in the process. Each iteration of development is relatively short, between two to four weeks, progress can be measured in small bursts, and the overall application is tuned and tweaked at the completion of each of these "sprints."

Automated scripting tools

Tools such as Chef and Puppet have been created to allow companies and users to take advantage of DevOps principles by quickly building out automated processes without having to be a skilled developer.

Automation

This is the act of taking a manual process or processes, typically performed by a person, and using technology to automate some or all of the process. It is typically done to save significant time, as well as to reduce the possibility of human error.

Back door

A back door in a system is used to provide an alternate method into an application or system. Some manufacturers put back doors into their systems so they can always get in, even if a customer accidentally locks themselves out. When a hacker penetrates a system, one of the first things they usually try to do is to install some type of back door so that, even if they way they broke in the first time gets fixed, their hidden back door is there for them to use again in the future.

BCP - Business continuity plan

A business continuity plan ensures that an organization knows what to do in the unlikely event a disaster strikes. If the building burns down, where do people go to work? How do they access their information? Who is responsible for contacting all employees, the press, the insurance company, etc.? The

BCP is the business bible, every organization should have one; most organizations don't.

Bolt-on security fixes

In typical software development, security isn't always tested at all, and many times when it is it ends up being done right before an application goes live. No one wants to delay the go-live date, so if/when security weaknesses are identified, many times some temporary security "fix" is bolted on to the application to try to address the problem. If security is added at the end, it's much easier for a malicious user to work around something that's bolted on vs something that is part of the foundation of the application.

Breach

When a computer system is broken into and information is stolen, it is commonly referred to as a breach.

Build books

When setting up a server or a network or security device, a build book is a set of procedures that should be followed each and every time a new system is being added to the network. The build book helps ensure consistency when setting up new systems, and should help to minimize risk exposures by identifying and eliminating unnecessary services and applications that may be installed by default.

Cost benefit analysis (CBA)

A systematic approach to estimating the strengths and weaknesses of various alternatives to satisfy functional requirements and benefits for a project or decision.

Cloud services

Services made available to users on demand via the Internet from a cloud computing provider's servers as opposed to being provided from within a company's own on-premise servers. Most businesses use cloud services for routine operations like hosting because of its ease of use and relative low cost.

Code reuse

When developing software, it is very common for developers to reuse lines or sections of code they have created to save time, ensure consistent performance and end results within the application. If the code they are reusing has any security weaknesses, they end up spreading that weakness into many different parts of the application, introducing new weaknesses and vulnerabilities in each place they are used.

Compliance

In general, compliance means conforming to a rule or set of rules such as a standard or set or regulatory requirements. Many organizations seek and attain "check box compliance," which in no way means they are secure, it simply means that they were able to satisfy the requirements of the standard they were hoping to achieve. With check box compliance, many companies think they are "done" when they get all the items in the standard checked as complete. In information security, you're never done, it's an ongoing, continuous set of activities that are never complete.

Cyber intrusion

A cyber intrusion is a break-in to a system through a network, rather than through a more conventional physical access path such as a door or window.

Cybersecurity

Also known as IT security, InfoSec, Information Security, computer security, it's the protection of information systems from theft or damage to the hardware, software, or the information stored on them.

Darknet

An underground or hidden network on the internet, typically used by hackers or malicious users to hide their activities from regular internet users and to conduct illegal business or share illicit information.

Data dump

A large amount of data all collected together in a single file or a collection of files in a single location.

DevOps

A combination of Development and Operations, it's a practice that emphasizes communication and collaboration between software development and other IT professionals, particularly those in IT operations. It has a focus on automation for software delivery and infrastructure changes, bringing the discipline of software deployment to regular IT operations.

Dynamic code analysis

This analysis is done against a running application. It is focused on finding security flaws and weaknesses in the way different features and functions have been implemented, and encourages the tester to do things within the application that a user wouldn't normally do to try to get the system to exhibit behaviour (such as showing information that it shouldn't) that is outside that expected from the application when operating normally

External security audit

Typically performed by an external third party, an external audit helps you understand what your organization's risk posture looks like from the outside, or at least from the perspective of someone from outside your organization. Some regulatory standards such as PCI, NERC CIP and others require at least an annual external audit to help identify potential weaknesses and risk exposures.

Firewall

A firewall is like a traffic cop, watching all communication into and out of a company's network. It makes yes or no decisions on whether to allow traffic to pass or to block it, based on a pre-defined set of rules.

Gold image

Just like in the record industry, the Gold Image is the final image that all other systems are created from. This image should be hardened (meaning all potential security problems like unnecessary running services, open ports are disabled or removed). When new security patches become available, the gold image should be patched and then a new version created to ensure all new systems being set up don't contain security weaknesses from unpatched vulnerabilities.

Internal security audit

Many corporations have an internal auditing team. Their focus is on testing and validating that any and all standards that the company is required to adhered to are being met and are in compliance. They may perform spot audits throughout the year, and typically will be responsible for preparing the organization and working closely with any external auditors.

IPS intrusion prevention systems

An IPS (or IDS in the case of a detection vs prevention system) is used to provide additional security controls for traffic entering and leaving a network. The IPS looks at the traffic and tries to determine if it is legitimate normal traffic or if there are patterns or behaviour that indicate the traffic is coming from someone or some source that is trying to do something malicious or unauthorized on the network. An IPS can actually block the connection, an IDS can only identify it and alert on it.

ISO 27001

One of the most well recognized information security standards. It is a specification for measuring and evaluating how well an organization's ISMS (Information Security Management System) is performing.

Malware

Malware is software that gets installed onto a system to do something that the system owner wouldn't want it doing. This could involve simple things like redirecting your search results to a certain location no matter what you search for, or could steal all your banking information and send it out to a server on the Internet to be harvested by a malicious user. Malware is sometimes very difficult to detect, and even once discovered can be difficult to remove completely from an infected system.

Mobile app

An application built and designed to be used on a handheld or portable device such as a smartphone or phablet, or on a tablet.

MSSP - Managed Security Services Provider

A company who takes responsibility for managing information security on behalf of its clients.

MVP - Minimum Viable Product

When doing development, especially in the Agile world, MVP helps you understand when a product is ready to be used by your end users. You may have designed an application with 100 features, but determine that only 20 of them are required to meet your MVP. Once they are all completed you can go "live" with your application, and continue to work on the remaining features while the application is in production, rather than waiting for the remaining 80 features to be completed.

NERC CIP

The North American Electric Reliability Corporation Critical Infrastructure Protection. This is a set of standards designed to protect and ensure the reliability of the North American bulk power system. It is a set of requirements that all utilities in the USA are tested against every 12-15 months. While not yet mandated in Canada, numerous Canadian utilities are actively pursuing NERC CIP compliance today, understanding that it is only a matter of time before Canada adopts the same mandated requirements.

Network architecture

This is the design of a communication network. It normally outlines the network's physical components as well as their functional organization and configuration, provides operational principles and procedures, and may dictate data formats to be used in operations.

Open source

Computer software with its source code made available with a license in which the copyright holder provides the rights to study, change and distribute the software to anyone for any purpose. It typically requires that the original creator of the open source code is given some type of reference or acknowledgement.

Patching

Patching is the most critical activity that an IT department can do to help minimize security risks and exposures. When you patch a system, you are applying a fix, normally provided by the manufacturer, to the system that has been identified as having a security hole. The patch is supposed to remove the security vulnerability from the system entirely, thereby reducing the risk exposure.

PCI-DSS or PCI

Payment Card Industry Data Security Standard, typically shortened to PCI. This is a standard created by the major credit card companies designed to enhance security. It applies to all retailers who take credit cards payments either online or in their establishments and who are connected to the Internet.

Penetration test

A penetration test takes up at the end of a vulnerability assessment. Rather than just finding the vulnerabilities, during a penetration test an attempt is made to use one or more of the identified vulnerabilities with a goal of compromising the system. Success from a pen test may be demonstrating access into a vulnerable system, it may be elevating privileges to be able to do things that an administrator can do, it may involve taking information off of a system, it may involve rendering the system unusable, or it may involve a combination of some or all of these results.

Perpetual auditing

Unlike the internal or external audit, which are considered "point in time" audits, the perpetual audit is just that, a continuous audit. This can be accomplished by implementing sufficient monitoring into a corporate environment so that there is visibility into what's happening on systems on an ongoing basis, and by implementing automated rules which perform a lot of the same checks the auditors would do during an annual audit, but are being performed all the time.

Peter Principle

This idea is that people are hired based on their effectiveness in their current role rather than their aptitude for their new position being considered. As a result of this, many employees find themselves advancing to positions they are not qualified for as a result of their record of prior competence. Under the

Peter Principle, managers "rise to their own level of incompetence". The theory was formulated by organization expert Laurence J. Peter.

PII - personally identifiable information

PII relates to information such as a person's address, social insurance number, health card number, where having access to all of that information together could be used by a malicious user to impersonate the person.

Plug-in

Typically a small piece of software that's designed to perform a specific function or functions as part of a larger application or service.

POS point of sale

A POS system is typically used in restaurants and retail stores to perform retail transactions. It can be used to accept cash, cheques, or credit card payments for goods being purchased.

RCMP integrated technology crimes unit (ITCU)

"C" Division Integrated Technological Crime Unit (ITCU) includes police investigators and civilian members and is responsible for investigating computer crimes of national or international scope and providing technical assistance to other investigative units. The ITCU investigates offences such as unauthorized access to a computer or computer network (computer intrusion or hacking), mischief in relation to data (theft, manipulation, deletion, etc.), and possession of equipment or passwords facilitating this type of offences.

Reporting metrics

Also called KPIs or Key Performance Indicators, these measurements are used to evaluate performance of a particular item or item. In the security world, KPIs could be used to measure the number of viruses detected over time, the number of attacks blocked at the firewall or at the IPS, the number of users connecting by VPN, etc. The goal is to use this information for both up-to-date as well as historical trending purposes.

ROI Return on Investment

In the IT world, ROI is used to help justify the purchase of tools or technologies in order to help improve security, streamline operations, save time and resources. An ROI may look at the cost of a tool and one-time implementation costs and compare it to the cost of having a person do the same work manually over a period of time to determine which is more cost effective.

Router

A router is a device which is plugged into your network and is responsible for directing traffic into, out of, and around on the corporate network. It may also have some basic firewall capabilities, making decisions on what traffic to "route" between one location or another and what traffic to block.

Run books

Once a system has been set up using a build book and has been added to the network, a run book provides guidance on its ongoing operations. The run book should provide details about how often a system should be scanned for vulnerabilities, when and how patches should be installed, and other items related to regular maintenance of the system.

Runtime compiler

A compiler is a computer program that takes source code and converts it into binary code, which is what most computers run in the form of applications.

SANS CSC Critical Security Controls (formerly SANS Top 20)

The CIS Critical Security Controls are a recommended set of actions for cyber defense that provide specific and actionable ways to stop today's most pervasive and dangerous attacks. A principle benefit of the Controls is that they prioritize and focus a smaller number of actions with high pay-off results. The Controls are effective because they are derived from the most common attack patterns highlighted in the leading threat reports and vetted across a very broad community of government and industry practitioners.

SaaS Software as a Service

A software licensing model where software is hosted centrally and licensed on a subscription basis to end users. Many businesses buy software under the SaaS model.

Scripts

A script is usually a set of instructions provided to a computer to get it to do something. Combining a script and a scheduler allows many organizations to implement some level of automation, where a script is run on a pre-determined schedule to accomplish one or more pre-defined tasks.

SDLC software development lifecycle

Any company that develops software should have some type of SDLC. This tells them how they should architect, design, and code their software to ensure it's developed in a consistent, reliable, repeatable and secure fashion.

Software deployment

Periodically, as new versions of an application are being developed, they must be deployed into production. The process of updating current software or of rolling out new software is referred to as software deployment. DevOps can help to significantly reduce the workload of software deployment and can help to assist in automating and improving the rollout.

Source code repository

This is a collection of all of the source code for your software. It allows all your developers to "check in" their code, helping to keep it organized. It may also help with tracking versions, bug tracking, release management, and documentation.

SSL secure sockets layer

Most web traffic today is being done using SSL. This is a cryptographic protocol which is designed to provide secure communications between two systems over a network. In web browsing, you typically see it used when doing things like banking and email communications. You know if SSL is active by looking for the lock icon in the top of your browser.

Standard imaging

Rather than setting each computer or server up inside an organization individually, a standard imaging process allows an organization to define what a typical system should look like, what applications should be installed, and then a "gold image" is created that can be used to set up additional systems using the image as a template.

Static code analysis

This is performed against an application's source code to look for weaknesses in the code itself. It is typically done against uncompiled code.

Switch

A switch is used to connect two or more devices together on a corporate network. With the advent of high-speed wireless there is a move to use more and more wireless connections, however the switch is still a well-established device in most corporate networks today. From a security perspective, if you compromise a switch you could intercept all traffic flowing between systems on the network, block traffic, and redirect traffic.

TCP ports

Most communication on the Internet is done using the Transport Control Protocol, or TCP. Every time you talk to a web server or check your email, the application you're running is making a connection to one or more TCP ports that are "listening" on the server you're connecting to.

Validation metrics

Validation metrics help an organization understand if something they are supposed to be doing is actually being done, and done effectively. An example would be where a company has a regulatory requirement to have anti-virus software installed on every machine. A validation metric may measure how many machines there are in the organization in total, how many of them have the anti-virus software installed, how many have the software actually running and not just installed, how many viruses have been detected and blocked, etc.

Version control

When building software, each time there is an update to the application, a new version is created. It is imperative that software developers use some type of version control so that if there are new bugs when new software is deployed, or if something stops working, they can roll back to a previous version or at least know under which version a security weakness or bug was introduced into the application.

Virtualized environment

Rather than running the operating system directly on a computer or server, it is run inside a virtualized environment using something called a hypervisor. This means that instead of one server having one application running on it, virtualization could allow one server to run many different "VMs" or virtual machines, with each machine using some of the physical server's CPU, memory and storage, maximizing the performance capabilities of the server

Vulnerability

A vulnerability is a weakness identified inside a system that, if exploited, could result in a malicious user gaining unauthorized access to the system, or could allow them to affect the performance of the system which contains the vulnerability.

Vulnerability assessment

A vulnerability assessment is designed to let an organization know about all the security weaknesses that exist in their systems and on their network. A tool or tools are run to find all of the devices, and then each device is scanned and the tool attempts to identify any known vulnerabilities based on a library of published vulnerabilities. In this type of test, there is no attempt to actually exploit any weaknesses identified, the goal is simply to document them and provide any evidence to confirm wherever possible they are real.

WAF web application firewalls

Web application firewalls provide an additional layer of protection for web-based applications. In many cases, they look like the application to the outside world. When you connect to a web application protected by a WAF, you're actually connecting first to the WAF; it looks at your connection request, decides if it looks like a normal request, and if yes allows you to connect on to the web application, all transparent to you, the end user.

Waterfall development model

Waterfall is a sequential design process for building software, where all aspects of the application are considered and fully understood before any software development is undertaken. It is highly structured and planned in order to avoid any changes during the development process. In Waterfall, it's not unusual to see a project take 1 year or 18 months, and in many cases much longer, before an initial product is ready for use by end users.

Wireframes

When developing an application, wireframes allow the developers to see what the application is supposed to look like and how it is supposed to function. They are essentially mock-ups of the application. Typically product management or a BA (business analyst) is responsible for creating the wireframes.

ABOUT THE AUTHOR

Dave Millier is one of Canada's most well-known and respected experts in the field of Information Security and Compliance. Dave is the founder of Sentry Metrics, a company that was widely recognized as one of Canada's leading Managed Security Service Providers. While at Sentry, Dave developed the award-winning Risk and Compliance Management platform, theSentry. After selling Sentry Metrics in 2014, Dave continued the development of the platform and relaunched and rebranded it Uzado (www.uzado.com).

Dave has been speaking internationally for many years at network and security conferences including Network World, Comdex, InfoSecurity Canada, SC Congress, and Canada's largest IT Security Education Conference, Sector. Dave is a recognized leader in risk management, and has helped some of Canada's leading organizations build and implement their corporate security strategies.

When he's not pursuing his plans for world domination (one client at a time), Dave is an avid motorcycle rider, and recently launched an off-road training school called Canada Rides (www.canadarides.com) where they teach safe dirt bike and ATV riding to riders of all ages.

INTERESTED IN LEARNING MORE?

Dave Millier, the author of this book, provides consulting services and would be very interested in having a discussion with you on any aspect of this book, or around information security in general.

Dave is the CEO of Uzado (www.uzado.com) and the CSO of Quick Intelligence (www.quickintel.com).

Dave's personal website is www.davemillier.com, where he can be booked for speaking engagements.

Dave can be reached any time at dmillier@uzado.com. He looks forward to hearing from you!

Made in United States
Troutdale, OR
11/03/2026

56844631R00130